SPEAKING WITH AN AUDIENCE

Speaking with an Audience

COMMUNICATING IDEAS AND ATTITUDES

JOHN J. MAKAY
The Ohio State University

HARPER & ROW, PUBLISHERS
New York   Hagerstown   San Francisco   London

SPEAKING WITH AN AUDIENCE: Communicating Ideas and Attitudes

Library of Congress Cataloging in Publication Data
Makay, John J
  Speaking with an audience.
  Bibliography: p.
  Includes index.
  1. Public speaking. I. Title.
PN4121.M317   1977   808.5'1   76-57960
ISBN 0-690-00897-X

To Mary, Elizabeth, and Kathryn

CONTENTS

Preface   *xi*

Chapter 1
Introduction to Public Speaking   *1*

The Speaker-Audience Relationship   *2*
Relevancy of Public Speaking   *3*
Speaker-Audience Relationship Models   *5*
Public Speaking as Rhetorical Process   *10*
Rhetorical Purpose and Effectiveness in Communication   *11*
The Communicator's General Objectives   *14*
The Speaker and the Message   *17*
Summary   *19*
Notes   *20*

Chapter 2
The Speaker: Control, Projection, and Ethical Dimensions   *21*

Speech Tension   *22*
The Speaker Projects Effectively   *30*
Delivery Is Nonverbal Communication   *31*
Crucial Behaviors for Communicators   *34*
Speakers' Dress   *37*
Nonverbal Distractions   *37*
The Voice and How To Use It   *38*
The Ethos of the Speaker   *43*
Ethos and Ethics   *45*
Summary   *48*
Notes   *50*

Chapter 3

Understanding Audience Behavior   53

Rational versus Psychological Persons   54
Understanding Information Processing in Audiences   59
The Psychology of the Audience   62
Major Audience-Centered Questions   70
Dominant Life-Style Factors   73
Important Kinds of Audiences   76
Summary   81
Notes   84

Chapter 4

The Speech: Stating a Proposition and Obtaining Information for Support   85

A Proposition Is the Core Idea   86
Unsupported Propositions   88
Research Supports the Proposition   89
Support for Clarification and Proof   89
Visual Support   99
"Attitudes" Are Important Supports   105
The Library   105
Audiovisual Materials Available in the Library   113
Taking Careful Notes   120
Tour the Library Completely   121
Personal and Secondary Experience as a Resource   121
Summary   126
Notes   127

Chapter 5

The Speech—Reasoning and Organization   129

The Toulmin Approach   130
Organization Is a Key to Effective Communication   139
An Effective Introduction   142
An Effective Conclusion   143
Three Models for Organizing a Speech   144
Preparing an Outline   148
Summary   152
Notes   154

Chapter 6
The Use of Words for Intended Meaning   155
Language: Word-Thought-Thing   157
Statements Invite Responses   160
We Project a Self-Image through Words   161
Audience Adaptation and Selection of Language   162
Personal and Social Meaning   163
Two Primary Levels of Language Sharing   164
Word Choice Is Crucial   167
Words Express Experience   168
Making Language Successful and Effective   171
Summary   172
Notes   173

Appendix A
A Special Assignment with Speeches   175
The Feminist Revolution, *Gloria Steinem*   177
National Health Insurance—Opportunity for Action Now,
    Leonard Woodcock   189

Appendix B
A Recapitulation of Course Objectives   200
Suggested Speech Communication—Messages   201

Selected Books for Additional Reading   210

Index   213

PREFACE

This book has emerged from a decade of teaching a basic course in communication that emphasizes speaking with an audience. Most of the information given here has been used effectively with students in the course, and with business and professional people who have had minimal or no previous training in speaking before an audience. The student is introduced to theories, concepts, and principles which may be applied in speaking situations on and off the campus.

While this book can best be used in courses that emphasize improvement of public speaking skills, it should also meet the needs of the instructor who wants *compact* and *concise* textual material for a speech communication course. It may be used by itself or with one or two paperbacks. In my class, additional readings about rhetoric and communication are used as supplements.

Before moving into the first chapter, twelve primary needs for speakers are listed. The book is addressed to helping speakers fill these needs.

Chapter 1 orients the student to the study and practice of speaking before an audience—why public speaking is both useful and relevant today. General objectives and basic communication models are used to introduce the student to the speaker-audience relationship in a rhetorical setting. Rather than divide speaking into discrete categories of speeches to inform, persuade, and entertain, I refer to the aims of a speaker as adoption, continuance, discontinuance, deterrence, exposition, and pleasure.

Chapter 2 focuses on the speaker and the problems of speech tension, delivery, ethos, and credibility. The purpose here is to identify the initial needs of a student in a theory-based skills course, and to help her or him to become comfortable at the outset of the course. The student is given a practical definition of speech tension, and a discussion of the symptoms, causes, and ways to minimize or eliminate it. The appropriate use of body and voice for effective projection is dealt with next.

Because tension and delivery are on the mind of the novice, these matters are discussed early in the book. In addition, the student is offered information about gaining the attention and acceptance of an audience through positive ethos and credibility.

Understanding audience behavior is the concern of Chapter 3. A discussion of the audience is necessarily more abstract than many aspects of speech construction, so this chapter may seem more theoretical than those which follow. How people behave as listeners and how one can analyze a group of listeners are crucial matters to the student of public speaking. Using a psychological approach, looking at information-processing, and dealing with attitudes, beliefs, and values are topics covered in this chapter.

Chapters 4, 5, and 6 show the student how to put a speech together. Forming a proposition, choosing support, conducting research, reasoning with ideas, organizing information, outlining, and finding the best words to create the intended meaning are discussed.

Chapter 4 tells the students how to select and state a proposition aimed at a specific purpose, what kinds of support are available to the speaker, and how she or he should conduct research. The student is introduced to propositions of fact, value, and policy, and practical examples are given. The library is given considerable attention; and the student is also encouraged to make use of other means of research—conversations, interviews, radio, television, and lectures.

Chapter 5 focuses on reasoning with an audience, and on the

organization of ideas, including how to prepare an outline. Traditional ways of organizing a speech are given, along with three basic models. One of the unique features of any speech is its language. Clarity or ambiguity, feeling or the lack of it—in a word, *meaning created for an audience*—depend upon the speaker's choice of words. Chapter 6 is devoted to this topic and to the role of language in the communication of ideas and attitudes. At the end of the chapter are 10 practical suggestions for the use of words.

Because instructors often prefer to choose their own activities for speaking and listening experiences with students, the activities in this book do not deal primarily with discussion questions and speech activities. Instead, the Appendix includes a copy of the syllabus for a multisection course called "The Communication of Ideas and Attitudes," which I teach to over 1000 students each year. Having participated in several basic conferences in the past year, I have seen many outlines which have a great deal in common with mine, and I am led to hope that *Speaking with an Audience* may be useful in many basic speech courses.

Primary Needs for Speaking with an Audience

The twelve primary needs of speakers may be given under three major headings: the speaker, the audience, and the speech.

THE SPEAKER

1. I need to develop realistic and desirable goals.
2. I need to handle my nervousness when I speak in public.
3. I need to develop a confident physical presence and vocal quality.
4. I need to have the audience accept and believe in me.

THE AUDIENCE

1. I need to understand the audience and how it relates to me and my speech.
2. I need to understand how the audience will perceive me and my speech.
3. I need to know how to relate my speech and myself to the audience.
4. I need to get information about my audience to help me develop my speech.

THE SPEECH

1. I need to learn how to conduct research for a speech.
2. I need to learn to use my research findings and my personal ideas and other information effectively.
3. I need to learn to state a main idea, reason with an audience, and organize my ideas with care and effectiveness.
4. I need to find the right words to create interest and meaning in my speaking.

Speaking effectively with an audience requires a sound understanding of the process and principles of public speaking, as well as practice and experience in using this understanding. Success in public speaking can bring great satisfaction. Good, effective speaking and listening skills can be learned. Some may learn the skills with more ease than others, but everyone can learn to improve as a communicator.

SPEAKING WITH AN AUDIENCE

CHAPTER 1

INTRODUCTION TO PUBLIC SPEAKING

Human beings are not the only living creatures who use sound and gestures for purposes of communication. But humans are the only creatures who have developed the sophisticated idea of communicating through verbal and nonverbal means. They have both the physical and the psychological capacity for emotional and intellectual activity, and can understand, persuade, make decisions, and give pleasure in this way. Humans are equipped with the mechanisms for verbal production and auditory reception. For eons people have spoken to each other, using the medium of language to convey meaning.

Attempts to improve human communication through the use of language (verbal and nonverbal) brought about the study and teaching of rhetoric, the art of using words effectively in speaking or writing. This study has centered on public speaking. We have evidence that the ancient Egyptians wrote about the principles of rhetoric over three thousand years ago.

Traditionally, the history of rhetoric begins with the study and practice of rhetorical communication in ancient Greece, the citadel of democracy in Western civilization, where free speech prevailed for hundreds of years. Thus the study of speech communication is grounded in a tradition begun thousands of years ago.[1]

The Speaker-Audience Relationship

From the writings of the earliest rhetorical theorists and practitioners to the present, one primary focus in speech communication has been on the relationship between the public speaker and the audience. Yet today it is not uncommon to hear individuals question the importance of learning the principles of public speaking. They ask: Why study and practice public speaking when people don't make speeches anymore? Is this true? Research indicates that people "make speeches" more often than we might think. Kathleen Kendall found some answers to the question: Do real people ever give speeches?[2] Her research indicates that members of the blue-collar class frequently speak to audiences of 10 or more people. She states: "Since those with more education spoke most frequently, one can expect that more highly educated persons would give speeches more often."

The person with a college education can expect to make many speeches. In my work as a consultant I have found this to be the case. Professionals, ranging from country-club green superintendents to psychiatric nurses, often say that they need skill in public speaking as well as skills in other kinds of communication.

Today's study of speech communication has broadened beyond a preoccupation with public speaking,[3] although this continues to be important. A contemporary curriculum in speech communication usually includes interpersonal communication, small-group behavior, communication theories and models, business and professional speech communication, and mass communication.

People establish speaker-audience relationships in order to affect

the welfare of individuals, groups, and societies. *The principles of public speaking are also generalized to a variety of other contexts and experiences.* Essentially this means that the principles learned in public speaking can be applied to conversation, interviews, and other communicative experiences. A thorough communication-training program should include particular courses in these subjects.

Relevancy of Public Speaking

Effective public speaking is relevant to persons in all the professions and in all walks of life. Success or failure, happiness or sadness, satisfaction or discontent are often determined by what persons say and do, why they speak and listen, how they communicate with each other, and how they respond as communicators. We can see this in our own lives and by observing the lives of others.

Regardless of special interests, people cannot escape the relevancy of public speaking. Instead of wondering how to relate a school subject to the needs of students, as can happen with some

courses, students of public speaking can often see an immediate application for this skill.

Someone who is hesitant or frightened about taking a "speech course" is usually worried about speech tension. We will deal with tension and fright in Chapter 2. It is not relevancy that bothers some students faced with taking a course in public speaking; it is nerves!

A course in public speaking can help in achieving a number of objectives, but three major goals are essential for improving communication behavior. The study and practice of public speaking can—

1. guide a person to a basic understanding of the process of speech communication;
2. help a person to prepare and present messages effectively for public and private occasions;
3. lead a person to develop critical thinking and listening skills.

These objectives should be a part of any introduction to public speaking. This book has been written to assist you in reaching these goals.

Speaker-Audience Relationship Models

The study of public speaking includes consideration of models which help us understand the process of communication. The development of our skills as speakers and listeners naturally follows our understanding of this dynamic process.

A model of communication is a description, often diagrammed, that calls attention to a part of the process of communication. Though we know that communication is not a static state, we must rely on charting the communication in order to gain an understanding of the process. This might seem to contradict the notion of process, but by breaking down the whole into parts we can come to understand the dynamics of the communication process. The three models presented on the following pages illustrate particular processes in public speaking. The first is basic to our study.

People base their public speeches on their perceptions. Perception is a process by which we sense, identify, classify, and create meaning for the stimuli we experience. If we put a finger on the stove, the sense of touch tells us whether it is hot or cold. A shadow seen in a dark corner may look like a shadow or like a lurking thief. One way for us to consider perception is to study and discuss a model of perception (see Fig. 1-1).[4]

The diagram seems to be complex. But the ideas it presents are important, and it is worth studying for several minutes. Now consider as an example the speech delivered by a member of a high-school graduating class. We will focus on one particular listener, a grandfather named Lloyd.

Judy is the first member of a graduating class to deliver a commencement speech at Springport High School. Previously a community leader had always been asked to speak at graduation, but this year the school administration, in cooperation with the senior class, decided to choose a student in open competition to deliver the commencement address. The selection panel chose Judy, whose speech was entitled "Moments to Remember." Judy designed the speech to recall the most important moments shared by the class during their school experiences.

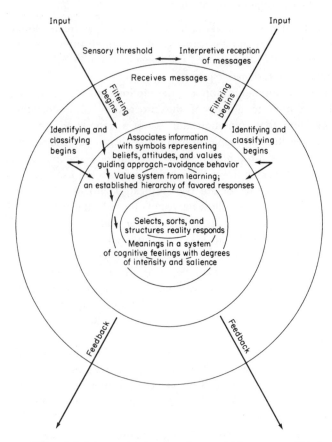

Figure 1–1. A human basic perception model for persons. This is what happens to information when you perceive and act as a communicator.

Lloyd is listening to Judy. He is very proud of his granddaughter Vicki. In his memory of the many commencements he has attended, Lloyd recalls only distinguished adult speakers. Consequently, he is puzzled at listening to a student instead of the community leader he expects to hear.

As Judy speaks about "moments to remember," Lloyd listens and receives impressions of what is taking place. What goes on in his mind and body, his reactions to the speaker and her speech begins with Lloyd's senses—his ability to see, hear, taste, touch, and smell. These senses make up a person's sensory threshold.

The commencement program is taking place out-of-doors, and the evening is warm and humid. Lloyd feels refreshed at being outside, but he is vaguely uncomfortable in his hard chair and he also feels crowded. The setting is for him both positive and distracting.

Judy's voice does not project well, and so Lloyd misses some of her words. As he strains to hear better, Lloyd's mind wanders to memories of his granddaughter growing up, for the speaker reminds him of Vicki. He pictures Vicki in his mind, and, his attention wandering, misses part of Judy's speech. When Lloyd does tune in, he *associates* Judy's words and her nonverbal behavior with *beliefs, attitudes,* and *values* which he already holds. He has seen several generations grow up, including his own. The views, appearances, and interests of his granddaughter's generation often puzzle him, at times anger him, at other times provide him with youthful joy. Now, as he listens, Lloyd *puts together in his mind* what he thinks Judy is saying, *creating meaning* for himself, giving importance to some views, less or almost no importance to others, and completely filtering out still others.

Each person in the audience is going through a similar process. And so, though there is one speaker and one speech, there are as many messages as there are people. There is the reality of the speaker's speech, and there are the perceptions of the members of the audience, each of whom hears the words of the speech and interprets them through a process of sensing, filtering, identifying, classifying, associating, valuing, and structuring. This is *perception,* a key to speech communication. Judy has written a speech and then presented it according to her perception of what she wanted to share with the audience.

Figure 1-1 shows how perception affects Judy's choice of words, expressions, and apparel for the occasion. Figure 1-2 is a comprehensive model of the public-speaking setting. Examine it carefully also, and then use the Springport commencement to remind yourself of the important elements and behaviors in the process of public speaking.

Judy is speaking not only for herself but as a representative of her class. When we speak before a group we do not operate alone or speak as a single voice. We represent an idea, an issue, or a group. When we speak "on the job" we represent our firms. When we speak on a controversial issue we represent others who share our views. When a person delivers a commencement speech, she represents the class as a whole as well as herself.

In the process of communication, a public speaker initiates message-sharing by designing a speech which will create similar meanings for everyone in the audience. Keep in mind that *meaning is what happens between two statements*. It is a kind of sensing of the identity between two statements. Meaning is a recognition of relationship; it is the perception that takes place when we capture the relationship between two statements. *In order to make such a relationship, each person must draw from his or her intellect and feelings, where attitudes, beliefs, and values are grounded as self-knowledge.*

Attitudes are predispositions about something or someone. *Beliefs* are degrees of faith. Values are deep inner anchors which guide us in our concepts of "good" and "bad." *Acquired knowledge* shapes our attitudes, beliefs, and values (intellect and feelings), and we reveal them in our verbal and nonverbal expressions. This is what happened when Judy prepared her speech. She created meaning for herself by choosing information centered in her attitudes, beliefs, and values. Then she structured this information into ideas through the use of language. Finally she shared her views in her speech.

To experience meaning similar to Judy's, each member of the audience would have to create within himself or herself symbols that they and Judy share. Each would receive the words; translate them; and respond according to the perception, attitudes, beliefs, and values that make up his or her intellectual and feeling self.

There are 285 persons in Judy's audience and each one creates "some message" within himself or herself. Judy has voiced her views

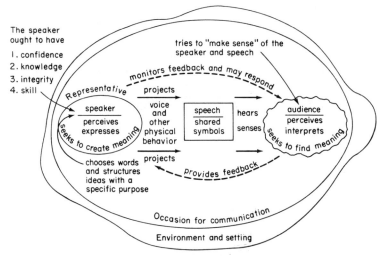

Figure 1–2. Basic model for speaking to an audience.

with a specific purpose in her mind, while the audience sees and hears according to its willingness and ability to listen and share.

Figure 1-2 suggests that a speaker's effectiveness with an audience depends on the speaker's confidence, integrity, knowledge, and skill, as well as the audience's predispositions, receptiveness, knowledge, and skill. It is important to realize that *full and free expression depends on the speaker's self-confidence* and his or her complete confidence in what is said.

To be believed by the audience, one must be seen as a person of integrity, a concept classical speakers wrote of as ethos or ethical standards. An audience will listen to a speaker who appears to know his or her subject and who can speak with skill. In order to create meaning, each listener will process what he or she perceives according to psychological predispositions about the speaker, the subject, and the occasion. The receptiveness of people in the audience to the speaker (a disgruntled parent in Judy's audience could tune her out with the thought: "The one thing I don't need is advice from an 18-year-old kid"), their knowledge relating to the subject, and their listening skill all affect meaning.

The speaker-audience relationship takes place on an occasion, and each occasion is centered in a geographical environment which is affected and generated by social, political, economic, and cultural norms and realities. What the speaker says and how the audience responds are determined to a great extent by both the occasion and the environment.

Public Speaking as Rhetorical Process

Traditionally, public speaking has been viewed and experienced as a rhetorical process. The question of what rhetoric is deserves a fuller discussion at this point.

According to speech authority Richard Crable, rhetoric has generally been defined in four popular ways:

1. Rhetoric can be hollow bombast, artificial eloquence, or style and form in speaking without content.
2. Rhetoric can be regarded as connoting dishonesty or deceit in communication.
3. Rhetoric can be exemplified in textbooks which deal with language use or composition.
4. Rhetoric can be the art and/or science of using language to persuade or influence.

But Crable proposed that "contemporary rhetorical study is concerned with symbolic interaction aimed at mediation. Rhetoric deals with how human beings settle differences between themselves and their environment; how they make 'their world' more the way they want it to be."[5]

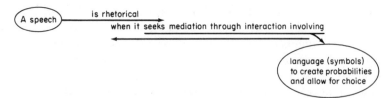

Figure 1–3. Public speech communication is a rhetorical process.

Most of us have ideas about the ways we would like to alter our world to make it a better place to live in. Certainly each of us has views about ways to change our colleges or universities to meet our needs in more satisfying ways. Our power is limited, but we have an instrument for change, if by that we mean mediation with others.

A speaker seeks to gain something by persuading an audience and choosing words that will sway the audience's point of view. *The audience chooses how to act.* Rhetoric can be instrumental for change by providing symbols to establish probabilities. These can be weighed and a choice then be made.

Rhetoric may be thought of as the process of human communication in which a speaker sorts, selects, and sends symbols for the specific purpose of evoking a precise response from the receivers. Used wisely, accurately, and clearly, symbols can create the understanding between a speaker and an audience that change is necessary and/or possible.

If there is an attempt at coercion there is no range of choice, and speech is not rhetorical. But when a speaker uses shared symbols to point out the best possible choice for the audience, the speech communication is rhetorical. This concept can be viewed more fully by examining the nature of rhetorical purpose.

Rhetorical Purpose and Effectiveness in Communication

Public speaking usually involves a rhetorical purpose If a supervisor tells his or her subordinates that they must follow company policy, then there are no alternatives from which the audience can choose in order to make a decision. The same is true if the ruler of a nation orders citizens to obey a law. The purpose of such messages is not rhetorical. On the other hand a rhetorical purpose can be met by adhering to the three criteria described below. When you use rhetoric in public speaking, you—

1. recognize that the attainment of the desired goal depends on the actions of other people;
2. seek from an audience the help needed to accomplish your goals by pointing out the choices available;

3. aim at achieving your goal voluntarily, relying mainly on shared symbolic transactions.

William Brown describes two types of rhetorical goals which are included in a rhetorical purpose: relationship goals seek to *adjust* human relationships. Task goals seek to *accomplish* ends.[6] For example, a good relationship must be established with your audience if you have to persuade them to support your position on an issue. The goal of establishing a good relationship is to win others to your cause. If a speaker's message focuses mainly on the *task*, on getting something done, he or she will be less successful than if relationship goals are pursued as well. Those in positions of power are more likely to be receptive to messages for change if the speaker pursues both relationship and task goals.

The speaker who says; "My listeners don't have to like me as a person in order to get the job done" is naive and is exercising poor judgment. Good human relationships are as important as a clear message. A teacher is more likely to create an effective learning environment if he or she includes both goals—good relations and clarity—in the lectures and discussions held in class. The same can be said for others who rely on speech communication for success in their professions.

For example, the administration of a small college, Dorian, had long, been opposed to drinking. A ban against drinking on campus had been maintained for some time. The majority of the students came from homes where social drinking was accepted, and so the students believed that drinking should be allowed on campus. A private poll revealed that most of the faculty members drank and also favored dropping the ban.

The president of Dorian College continued to affirm his and the college's stand against changing the rule. To allow drinking on campus, he contended, would impair the developing intellectual and moral growth of the students.

One spring morning, in the coffee shop, a group of students decided the time had come to initiate a change in the rules and to abandon an outmoded, old-fashioned prohibition. They began a movement to get the drinking ban changed. The method of change would be informative and persuasive discourse. These students thought that driving to town in order to drink, as they had been doing, was hypocritical. They formed an ad hoc organization called BEAR, an acronym for "better ethics are right." A date was chosen for a public rally at which one of the founding group would be the main speaker. Each student believed that persuasion through public speeches could be instrumental in effecting a change. The students planned to present a variety of speakers from several campus groups, all favoring the removal of the drinking ban. In order to achieve the aims of BEAR, relationship and task goals would have to be achieved with those in a position to influence change—the students, parents of students, alumni, and those college officials who were not morally opposed to social drinking. Members of BEAR had to raise the issue, rely on shared symbolic transactions, and mediate for change. If they had chosen violent actions instead of speaking out, the president might have reacted with a swift police crackdown and punishment. Nonrhetorical purposes would then have existed, and speech communication would have had no place in the events that followed.

To effect change or preserve the status quo, a lone speaker with a single speech is often ineffective. The three criteria for rhetorical purpose explain why. This is graphically rendered in Fig. 1-4. We do know that one speech can be highly effective in clarifying meaning and bringing about change, but the one speech is generally part of a continuing dialogue on a subject.

If we stand before an audience, for example, and argue that the press should not disclose and elaborate on the alleged intimate details of President John Kennedy's sex life, we are articulating views which are part of the flow of discourse on the subject. Our impact, or lack of it, is the result of this talk and other messages the audience has heard. We apparently stand alone for the moment, but the message is added to others from those who share our views.

We now turn to the general objectives and specific purpose for speaking. These are centered within the rhetorical purpose, with its relationship and task goals. If we are to be effective, each of us must

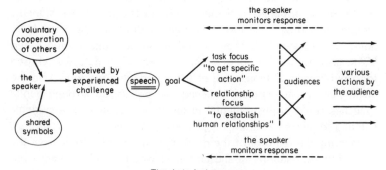

The rhetorical purpose

Figure 1–4. The rhetorical purpose.

have a general objective and specific purpose in mind as we prepare and present a speech.

The Communicator's General Objectives

Once a speaker has chosen a subject, she or he must decide on two things: (1) What is my general objective in speaking? (2) What is my specific purpose? Since the specific purpose of any message grows out of the speaker's general objective we can consider general objectives first.

The objectives of the speaker are concerned with effects. Effects in communication can be of two kinds: consummatory and instrumental.

> Consummatory effects are those receiver responses which engender immediate gratification. Laughter at a funny incident related by a communicator, or general chatter which takes place in a coffee shop among several friends who are relaxing before going to class are examples. An instrumental effect, on the other hand, includes those responses which serve a more lasting goal, which may be the speaker's specific goal. The specific goal of any speaker is the precise response he wants from his listeners.[7]

There are six general objectives in speaking: adoption, continuance, discontinuance, deterrence, exposition, or pleasure.[8]

Adoption. If the speaker is seeking to change the audience., the objective is adoption. For example, a city-planner from the State Department of Environment and Natural Resources appeared before an audience of city officials in an old, historic, and scenic city of 21,000 people to persuade them to support a proposal to renovate part of the city and develop a group of new parks. Many in her audience were resistant to change in the city's environment and were suspicious of the state official because she seemed quite young. She sought, through speech, to get the audience to adopt her proposal. Her presentation was successful.

Continuance. A speaker who seeks the maintenance of the status quo has continuance as an objective. If he or she believes that the direction in which the audience is going is correct, the speaker offers only information and inspiration to the audience. For example, if the affirmative action program of a large corporation is going well and meeting its goals, the only task of the AA officer, when speaking to corporate executives, would be to reinforce their commitment to the program and perhaps to expand it. The speaker wants the program to continue smoothly.

Discontinuance. If a speaker wants an audience to abandon a program or procedure, the aim is discontinuance. For example, when a new manager took over a chain of retail stores headed for eight years by another, one of his first messages was: "There is nothing wrong with abandonment. Some policies in this chain need to be discontinued." This speech was followed by others in which the speaker argued for continuing some policies and adopting new ones. Over a period of time he won his points.

Deterrence. When a speaker determines that an audience is about to face an undesirable experience or an impending crisis, or when the speaker believes an audience possesses something which the speaker sees as highly threatening or likely to result in disaster, he or she may try to bring about some sort of effective block to the threat or danger. For example, a representative of a new suburban community recognized that he and his neighbors had purchased homes in a community filled with young children of preschool and elementary school age. The local school system, however, appeared to lack adequate upper-level school facilities, which would eventually be needed to accommodate a future junior and senior high school population. Many of the man's neighbors talked of the probability of having to move to a different community when their children reached the teen years. A group was formed to canvass the school district and speak to gatherings of taxpayers about the need to plan new school facilities. Before the speakers argued in favor of a proposal, they sought to convince audiences that the school system faced an impending crisis because of limited educational facilities, a crisis that must be deterred. Once the initial speeches had been delivered, a new series was prepared, arguing for the adoption of a building program. The group had determined the most desirable sites for construction, and they advocated building the necessary high school facilities on these. The general objective of the first set of speeches was *deterrence*. The second series had *adoption* as the goal. Those in opposition to the aims of this group spoke in favor of *continuance*. These people believed that the current educational facilities were satisfactory and could accommodate any future growth in student population.

Exposition. There are many situations which call for speakers whose aim is to educate an audience by giving it information. This is the case, for example, with academic lectures, which are designed to present objective and factual messages that the audience can receive and apply in any way it wishes. That does not mean that an expository speech cannot be persuasive. A lecturer was informing her class about nutrition in the foods they eat. Because she believed college students frequently avoid breakfast, she explained various ways in which to prepare a healthy but quick morning meal. She declared her intentions to be purely educational. Yet four weeks after the lecture 50 percent of her students confessed they had been persuaded to eat granola for breakfast. Even the instructor had begun to have granola for breakfast.

The essential objective of exposition in a speech is information. Presented in a highly meaningful way this kind of speech can touch human motives and result in the achievement of one or more other objectives.

Pleasure. The United States is a nation of people who like to be entertained and to make speeches "just for the fun and pleasure of it." The speaker for pleasure seeks mainly consummatory effects, though on occasion the aims can be instrumental ones. A speaker may want to engage in verbal play, cause an audience to laugh, ease tensions, or provide some dramatic moments of storytelling. After-dinner speeches, for example, are messages aimed mainly at getting audiences to experience pleasure; they generally do not seek adoption, continuance, discontinuance, deterrence, or exposition. At other times pleasure is combined with one or more of the objectives we have been considering.

A women's group in a large metropolitan area annually sponsors a lecture series. The speakers are actors and authors who appear for a fee and talk lightheartedly in order to stimulate feelings of pleasure in the listening audience.

Recently a political figure in the news appeared at a banquet as a featured speaker. After about 12 minutes of nonpolitical one-liner jokes, he made a transition into the second phase of his message, which sought to get his audience to continue their support of their political party. The people had fun, and at the same time they were inspired to continue working for specific political goals.

The Speaker and the Message

After determining the topic of a speech, the objective the speaker wants to pursue, and the time allotted for the speech, the next step is determination of its specific purpose. *The specific purpose of any speech communication should be the precise response the speaker wants from an audience.* What does the speaker want the audience to do? Speakers do not control the minds of others, but they can take careful aim at a specific purpose and try to be as effective as possible in achieving it.

When a speaker stands before an audience, verbally wandering aimlessly through ideas he or she has not determined the objective and specific purpose of the speech. Given enough time, a speaker might have several purposes in mind, all of them consistent with his or her objectives. In a typical course in public speaking, however, a single message usually has one general objective and one specific purpose. A class assignment may be the preparation of a series of five-to seven-minute speeches on the same topic each student's speech having a different general objective and different specific purpose. Another way of handling practice in public speaking is to prepare speeches with several objectives and responses as goals. In a consulting role for an industrial organization's speakers bureau I guided my students in the preparation of four five-minute speeches, each on a topic centered in their work. At the end of the series each student blended the four speeches into one 25-minute speech for the speakers bureau. Each speech had one to three general objectives and several desired responses as its aim. In determining the specific purpose of a speech, the specific behaviors a speaker wants the audience to engage in can actually be written out. This book will guide the student in ways of achieving specific responses. *We should know what we want from an audience when we have it before us.*

When a swimming pool salesperson speaks to potential customers at a neighborhood meeting, he or she knows precisely what response is being sought. Selling a product for profit is a strong incentive to aim carefully—"I want the audience to purchase a pool for their community from my company, and, if possible, pools for their backyards as well." There are two separate steps to achieving the objective: (1) convince the audience they need swimming pools; (2) convince them that the speaker's swimming pools are the best buy. Purchase is the speaker's purpose!

Clear purpose is important to an audience as well as to a speaker. One afternoon some students were grumbling in the student union about their course in statistical research methods. Most of the comments can be summed up in the statement: "I know Dr. Burns is an intelligent person, but I am confused about his purposes in some of the lectures. He seems to get off the track a lot and go off on tangents which completely lose me, even though I am taking notes and reading the text." Perhaps the students are not sophisticated enough to understand the subject matter of the course, but more likely Dr. Burns is not certain about his specific purpose.

A visiting priest on the "Merv Griffin Show" once remarked that he was touring churches and listening to young priests speak. He told the viewers: "I have decided that if these young men had to sell insurance for a living they would probably starve to death." Could it be that they spoke without having determined their specific purposes for speaking?

Recently a scientist appeared before a group of colleagues in different but related fields. The scientist announced that he was going to talk about the nation's energy crisis, presenting a great deal of information some of which he hoped would stick in their minds. He blasted away for 30 minutes, rapidly firing highly technical terms and data at the audience, flashing complicated tables and charts on a screen, and rambling from one concern to another without logical pattern. The result was utter confusion on the part of the audience. After a critical discussion of the speaker and the speech, it became evident to *everyone* in the room that *no one* knew the specific purpose of the speech. A number of reasons were offered to explain why this had occurred. Most basic of these reasons was the speaker's lack of decision about his purpose.

SUMMARY

Public speaking has been a major force in creating human understanding and progress since the dawn of civilization. Though other forms of human communication have a key role in creating understanding and progress, the need for people to be able to stand before others and speak with ease, comfort, and purpose is paramount. Public speaking is relevant to the work and life-styles of today.

Students can profit from an understanding of the process of speech communication. They should develop skill in the preparation and presentation of messages for private and public rhetorical situations, skill in critical thinking and listening, and an appreciation of the importance of sound training in public speaking. To achieve these ends, understanding of key models for public speaking is essential. These key models include: Basic Perception, Public Speaking, Rhetorical Process, and Rhetorical Purpose.

Finally, general objectives and specific purposes must be clear if speakers are to impress and persuade an audience. General objectives usually include adoption, continuance, discontinuance, deterrence, exposition, and pleasure. The specific purpose of any message is the precise response sought by a speaker from an audience.

NOTES

1. For excellent study, see George Kennedy, *The Art of Persuasion in Greece* (Princeton: Princeton University Press, 1963). Also see M.L. Clarke, *Rhetoric at Rome: A Historical Survey* (New York: Barnes & Noble, 1963), and James J. Murphy, ed., *A Synoptic Historic of Classical Rhetoric* (New York: Random House, 1972).

2. Kathleen Kendall, "Do Real People Ever Give Speeches?" *Central States Speech Journal* 25 (Fall 1974): 233–35.

3. See Keith Brooks et al., "The Study of Communication," in *Exploration in Speech Communication,* ed. John J. Makay (Columbus: Charles E. Merrill, 1973), pp. 3–18.

4. "A Basic Perception Model" appeared originally in John J. Makay and Beverly A. Gaw, *Personal and Interpersonal Communication: Dialogue with Self and with Others* (Columbus: Charles E. Merrill, 1975), p. 40. Reprinted with permission from the publisher.

5. Richard E. Crable, "What Can You Believe about Rhetoric?" in *Exploration in Speech Communication,* ed. John J. Makay (Columbus: Charles E. Merrill, 1973), pp. 27–38.

6. John J. Makay and William R. Brown, *The Rhetorical Dialogue: Contemporary Concepts & Cases* (Dubuque: William C. Brown, 1972), p. 65–124.

7. Wallace C. Fotheringham, *Perspectives on Persuasion* (Boston: Allyn & Bacon, 1966), pp. 28–34.

8. John J. Makay and Thomas C. Sawyer, *Speech Communication Now! An Introduction to Rhetorical Influences* (Columbus: Charles E. Merrill, 1973), pp. 41–46.

CHAPTER 2

THE SPEAKER: CONTROL, PROJECTION, AND ETHICAL DIMENSIONS

We now focus on ourselves, as speakers, for we are a major element in the models of public speaking given in this book. Four of the most basic public-speaking needs are—

1. the need to handle nervousness when speaking in front of an audience;
2. the need to be confident in our appearance before an audience and to feel good about ourselves as speakers;
3. the need to improve vocal quality and physical behavior as speakers;
4. the need to be favorably received by an audience and have it believe in the honesty and integrity of the speaker.

In order to respond to the first two needs—handling nervousness and feeling good about ourselves—the discussion now turns to an analysis of speech tension, or stage fright.

Speech Tension

When asked what they expect to gain from a basic course in public speaking, most students answer that they expect to learn self-confidence, to "do away with the jitters," to speak before an audience "without being so nervous."[1] The best way to deal with speech tension is to define it and then examine its major symptoms and their causes. Once that is accomplished, we can study the best ways to cope with these symptoms.

Definition. Speech tension can be viewed as a *normal state of anxiety occurring in anyone confronted with a speaking situation in which the performance is important and the outcome is uncertain.*[2] Several parts of this definition warrant careful examination if we are to understand and cope with speech tension.

The first point is that such tension is a *normal* state of anxiety. Almost every public speaker has had speech tension; those who will speak in public in the future will experience it whether they are novices or experienced speakers. Even experienced performers and

actors like Paul Lynd and McLean Stevenson admit to experiencing performance anxiety regularly.

The second consideration is the existence of tension when a speaker is confronted with an *important* speaking occasion and the outcome is *uncertain*. When a speaker faces an audience, regardless of the rhetorical goal, he or she has no guarantee of effectiveness; public speaking, therefore, deals with a probability. A teacher hopes the students will learn certain principles after hearing a lecture; a political candidate hopes to win votes after speaking to an audience; the after-dinner speaker hopes to evoke laughter. But in each case the speaker must realize that some listeners will not learn; some will not vote; and some will not laugh. The outcome is uncertain. Regardless of anxiety because of the importance of the occasion and the uncertainty of the outcome, the speaker's tension can be made minimal. In fact, nervous energy can be put to positive use in making communication as effective as possible. To achieve relief from the primary symptoms of speech tension and its causes, a speaker must be able to recognize and deal with them.[3]

Physiological Symptoms. Probably the most disconcerting symptoms experienced by a tense public speaker are the physiological ones—the dryness of the mouth, shaking of the knees, quickening of the heartbeat, cracking of the voice. These are the same for anyone experiencing stress, even people who generally feel "okay." The symptoms are quite *normal* for public speaking occasions. Being overly concerned about experiencing them can lead to accelerating them, which only makes giving a speech a nerve-racking experience.

Negative Self-evaluation. A feeling of unworthiness about being a speaker is another primary symptom of speech tension. It can be expressed in the thought: "There must be at least 25 people in this room who could do a better job of speaking than me. What am I doing up here?" This is a self put-down which is usually unwarranted. Even accomplished speakers—though some do it with a sense of false humility—may indicate to the audience that they are not good speakers but delivering a speech is something that must be done.

An attorney who recently graduated from a law school said that he and many of his colleagues found delivering a 20-minute summation the least skillful thing they did as lawyers. This is a negative self-evaluation about being a public speaker, and whether a person is weak as a speaker or not, it is a common symptom of speech tension. Such negative beliefs will be disturbing to the speaker and will add to his or her tension.

Withdrawal Symptoms. Like the other primary symptoms of speech tension, withdrawal is often found in settings quite different from public speaking. A person faced with a threatening encounter may feel like avoiding the threat through attempted flight. The feeling can be so strong in a student new to the study of public speaking that he or she will become ill on the day of the speech or will sit anxiously in the student union building and miss class. This kind of behavior is unfortunate because it merely prolongs the problem.

Once in front of an audience, a speaker who is experiencing withdrawal may avoid looking at the audience by gazing around the room at the ceiling, the floor, out the window, or into a plug on the wall. An audience likes a speaker to look at them; it is not impressed with withdrawal. Even a speaker's voice can give evidence of withdrawal, as it slips into a dim monotone rather than the expected enthusiastic projection.

These three primary symptoms of speech tension are not mutually exclusive. They can operate simultaneously, though one symptom may be more dominant at a given moment than another. As an example, while speaking to a group of Kiwanians about his work in brain-cancer research, a veterinarian began to feel physiological symptoms. These reactions of his body led him to think: "Boy, I'm convinced speaking is not my thing." Soon he began looking at his notes, up in the air, and everywhere but into his audience.

Major Causes of Speech Fright. In general we can identify four major causes of the three symptoms we have been discussing:

1. an intense desire to be successful at speaking,
2. an approach/avoidance conflict within the self,
3. a feeling of inadequacy or poor self-image about being a speaker,
4. a distortion of the speech situation.

We have decided that public speech communication is a process centered on probability, and that there is some degree of uncertainty within both the speaker and an audience as to the speaker's effectiveness and achievement of a purpose. We also know that speakers want to succeed and accomplish their goals with an audience. Yet no one has a 100 percent guarantee of success, and each speaker must realize this fact.

Studies indicate that knowledge of how difficult public speaking is for us is a primary factor in nervousness.[4] One of the instructors of public speaking was approached by a young chemical researcher during a consulting seminar at a huge corporation. The researcher explained that his bosses did not perceive him to be highly concerned about his work because his formal presentations to them seemed to be unenthusiastic. But in reality he was so enthusiastic about his work that he wanted to achieve the highest level of success in speaking. He gave the appearance of lacking enthusiasm about his work because he severely experienced the three symptoms we have been discussing. His strong desire to succeed was definitely a major cause of his speech tension.

The approach/avoidance conflict within the self is a second major cause of speech tension. This conflict occurs when someone wants to come near to and at the same time avoid a specific goal. Approach/avoidance behavior is rather typical of the way speakers act. For example, a university staff member was asked by a department chairman to attend an evening program to introduce parents of commuting students to the university and the sort of orientation their children would receive as they entered school. The instructor gave his reluctant agreement, but when he arrived at the hot, humid, and crowded ballroom in the student union building, he felt the evening's program would be dull and physically uncomfortable. He wondered if it was really unnecessary for him to be there. He left the room, but after walking about 100 yards, he began to turn around. Nearing the union building again, he veered off toward a beer joint near the campus. Several moments later, feeling he really ought to attend the meeting as a representative of his department, he marched back into the building and joined in a "social mixer" where parents could meet professors from all the departments represented. Reviewing these incidents shows that the instructor dutifully approached the event and at other times intensely felt the urge to avoid it physically, mentally, and emotionally. The whole evening had been very stressful, frustrating, and unsatisfying. This example illustrates what often happens to a public speaker during the preparation and presentation of a message—he or she moves between feelings and actions of *approach* and feelings and actions of *avoidance*.

Speech tensions can result from the conflict of approach and avoidance. A student, required to take a course in speaking, may put off the requirement as long as possible, while realizing that this course is one he or she really has a strong need to take. Once into the course such a person musters up an enthusiasm for doing well in speech assignments and may also experience a wish not to attend classes. One student who was majoring in communication was absent for three of the five speeches she was to present in class. She handed in official-looking excuses from a campus physician indicating she had been at the campus health center. But when the pressure became strong and the time short for her to make up the missed speeches, she confessed to her teacher that she had actually missed her assignments because of an acute case of speech tension. She had *approached* the assignment and then *avoided* it during various stages of preparation. She would head for class with the completed speech notes in her purse, but then stop short of the building, feel ill, and go to the health center instead. Her approach/avoidance behavior was strong enough to make her experience symptoms of speech tension.

The feeling of inadequacy is a third primary cause for speech tension. An instructor in public speech communication spent several hours each month teaching recruiting officers in the armed forces how to prepare and present speeches for high-school students. Almost all the men and women in the consultation meetings over a 2-year period viewed themselves as inadequate to "give speeches," and admitted this caused much of their anxiety.

Have you ever heard a public speaker begin by apologizing to the audience? "I don't know why I've been asked to speak on this topic, because there certainly are far better qualified people than I," may be a typical opening. It is really an expression of inadequacy. At a conscious and/or unconscious level, which manifests itself both in the thoughts and the body sensations of a nervous speaker, is often a genuine sense of unworthiness, uncertainty, and lack of "speech skills" which add up to personal inadequacy.

A fourth major cause of speech fright is a distortion of the public-speaking situation. Distortion means a person's disproportionate, threatening, and inaccurate mental picture and emotional feelings about what is expected when facing an audience. Rob, a college freshman, was approached by a senior to appear as a guest speaker in his pulpit. The senior, Ralph, supported himself by serving as a pastor of a small church in a rural area near the college campus. He often asked students from courses on religion to be guest speakers on Sunday. Rob was considering a career in the ministry, but he was an inexperienced public speaker and he had never before spoken in public about his religious views. The mere fact of Ralph's invitation so paralyzed Rob that it took him a couple of minutes just to blurt out, "No—I can't do it." In his mind's eye Rob envisioned himself facing a large and pious crowd eagerly awaiting his message. In reality the church was a small building, and Sunday morning attendance was usually about 40 people from nearby farms. These were friendly people, eager for weekly fellowship, and they liked hearing guest speakers.

Several weeks after his first invitation Ralph again invited Rob to speak at the church. This time, with less anxiety, Rob agreed. He had failed to develop an accurate picture of what the speaking situation was to be like, and so he prepared a talk on the meaning of the story of the Prodigal Son for contemporary society. He also found his nervousness growing because of his "inner distortion" of the public speaking situation. Rob experienced tremendous relief when he accompanied Ralph to the church for the Sunday worship service. Instead of a mysterious cathedral with a threatening-looking audience, Rob found a small red brick church with about 40 friendly people inside. They liked him and they liked his message. Reflecting on the experience, Rob eventually confided to his speech teacher that the major cause of his anxiety seemed to have been a misinterpretation of the situation.

Running through all the cases we have examined is a major element which seems to be the root cause of speech tension—*self-consciousness*. Approach/avoidance behavior, the strong desire to succeed, the feeling of inadequacy, the distortion of the public speaking situation are all fueled by the anxiety of self-consciousness. It seems almost too simple to be true, but if each of us checks our own experience of speech tension we can see that anxiety, nervousness, and fear come out of thinking within ourselves. Our thinking should be about the task we hope to accomplish with our audiences. Research on speech tension bears this out.

The Key to Control. An understanding of speech tension is the first step to controlling it. We have examined the symptoms and causes of speech tension. If we can recognize, accept, and deal with these symptoms we can reduce the tension we feel. It is important to realize that being keyed-up is both normal and desirable for effective public speaking. One instructor tells his students that the speaker who is not keyed-up before a speech is probably "stoned or asleep." If you are totally relaxed, your speech will not get off the ground.

Because the major cause of speech tension is self-consciousness, the best method for controlling it is for the speaker *to focus on the task and not the self.* The statement is easy to make but hard to put into practice. It is, however, a primary principle for the control of speech tension. If the focus is on the task of relating to the audience and on the delivery of the message and not the self while preparing to speak in public distortion will be at a minimum in the speaking situation. We will not experience feelings of inadequacy. We will not conjure up a poor self-image. We will not experience the approach/avoidance shift in mind and body which makes the public speaking experience little or no fun—and certainly a drain on the nervous system. Physiological symptoms, negativism, and withdrawal will be relieved.

It seems as if some people can never get this principle internalized into their speech behavior. A student leaving a class in public speech communication gasped to her instructor: "Ahhh. Only one more speech to go! I sure will be glad when this is all over!" When the instructor discussed the statement with her, she became aware that she was still very much self-centered and had not yet become message/audience centered. *Becoming message/audience centered is the primary key to speech control.*

Two additional points should be mentioned if we are to deal effectively with speech tension. First, we should always remember that audiences are friendly. Admittedly there are exceptions to this principle, but *in general audiences approve of speakers, want them to succeed, and recognize their adequacy as speakers when they make the effort to speak effectively.* Second, anxiety lessens and can be controlled as experiences in public speaking increase in number.

In an effort to make this point with reticent naval recruiting officers, their public-speaking instructor told them not to sit around the office waiting for speaking invitations. They were advised to seek maximum experience in speaking by looking for audiences so that they could gain experience and serve their profession and themselves well. *Anxiety can disappear with experience.*

Finally, a speaker must be fully prepared in order to have self-confidence. Many students become self-conscious on the day they are to speak if they are not as prepared as they should be. The un-prepared speaker cannot succeed, is bound to feel inadequate, and certainly experiences approach/avoidance feelings. *The confident speaker is one who is fully prepared to speak.*

The Speaker Projects Effectively

In general, people seem to place a great deal of emphasis on the physical and vocal delivery of a speaker. Comments such as "She sure is a spellbinder when it comes to speaking" or "One thing you have to say for him is he certainly is a good speaker" are often heard. To be honest, one can compose eloquent sentences, use common sense, be logical, and do well in other facets of speech preparation; but failure to speak in a way appropriate to the occasion and attractive to the audience makes for minimal effectiveness. For example, a novice instructor in speech communication once declared to his officemate: "I'm not interested in teaching delivery in our public speaking course; I'm teaching people to reason and to think." Three weeks later he confessed: "I've got to turn things around because I've been listening to the most boring speeches I've heard in a long time. I'm going to begin working with my students on using their voices and gestural behavior to project reasons and language." The instructor's students had been largely ineffective as public speakers because of their weak deliveries.

No so long ago several thousand military men and women sat in battalions on the side of a hill while a two-star general droned on about his vision for the success of his command. His voice, aided by an electronic amplification system, was a dull monotone, and his body and eyes scarcely moved. One observer noticed how bored the audience appeared to be. An attorney recently lamented that he was leaving the courtroom scene for nonspeaking corporate work.

His reason was that he could not speak out in order to articulate what he knew and believed about his cases. The general and the attorney had one thing in common when it came to speaking: They were dull to listen to and watch, in spite of the value of their messages.

A group of volunteers spent an entire initial campaign meeting in a gloomy discussion of what a boring speaker their candidate was. One member of the group, an instructor in communication, took a campaign speech by the candidate to the instructor's university speech criticism course. He gave each student a copy of the manuscript and analyzed the things that made the speech sound, logical, well organized, and meaningful. Then he played a tape recording of the speech. The class agreed that the vocal delivery did not do anything for the speech. It was simply unattractive.

We cannot all be dynamic orators; but we can improve physical projection to its fullest potential.

Delivery Is Nonverbal Communication

Delivery is a significant factor in a speaker's success or failure at influencing an audience. Part of a speaker's effectiveness is determined by the visible and audible presentation of a message. Mark Knapp reminds us that "through the use of gestures and body movements, a spoken message is repeated. If an irate instructor orders a mischievous student to leave the room and then points to the door, we have a case of repetition of the verbal by the nonverbal."[5] This nonverbal communication operates through the sound of the voice, in the same way as with the movement of the body. When the basketball coach told his collegiate team they would fly to their away games on an aged but safe chartered D-C 3, the team captain said: "Aw right, coach, that sounds like added fun for the trip"; but the sound of his voice suggested fear, insecurity, and disappointment to the coach and his fellow players.

"The nonverbal elements of speaking communicate as do words and sentences. The speaker's voice reveals his ideas, health, and emotional condition, for instance. Happiness, fright, and illness may be indicated by the force, rate, and pitch of the voice. Whether or not the impression gained from the expression accurately communicates the way a speaker actually feels, an audience may get such an impression anyway."[6]

Charles Galloway suggests: "Everyday we say things without words that we'd rarely have the courage to say out loud."[7] Galloway cautions against the assumption that specific signs and expressions can reveal what a person is thinking or feeling. A dictionary of such signals is not available, but Galloway has compiled some bodily movements and their meanings:

1. Crossed arms may be a sign of relaxation, but if done suddenly, after a point has been raised, generally shows defensiveness.
2. Inappropriate laughter can show anxiety about inappropriate arguing.
3. Foot-wiggling by several members of a group is a sign that something is wrong.
4. Smiles with the mouth but not the eyes, quick and weak, denote annoyance.

The important principle to keep in mind in relation to delivery in public speaking is that there is meaning without words and there is a way of learning without linguistics. We want words to convey intended symbols so that the audience can recreate "our meanings" in "their understandings." In order to have the greatest probability of this happening, effective delivery which is completely consistent with verbal behavior must be used.[8]

> Nonverbal communication in delivery [can] enhance the speaker's effort to achieve a specific purpose. . . . There are movements and gestures which could definitely hamper effective communication. . . . Any posture, movement, or gestural behavior can be contributory if it does not draw attention to itself and away from the ideas central in communicating. Speaking in front of an audience calls for (poise), and/or balance, and symmetry. A poised speaker will distribute his weight equally and appear with the dignity to convey

self-assurance. He will also be relaxed and flexible enough to provide meaningful body movement and gestures.[9]

Facial Expressions. Research suggests that the expressions of the face have the greatest impact in affecting the meanings generated by words and vocal sound. A psychologist warns: "If the facial expression is inconsistent with the words, the degree of liking conveyed by the facial expression will dominate and determine the full impact of the message."[10] Others contend that " 'the most expressive part of the body is the face,' and this general view is symbolized by the way we use the word face as an idiom—'let's face it,' 'she lost face,' 'facing the problem is difficult,' 'it's just something we have to face.' "[11]

Imagine delivering an important speech to an audience of strangers. Picture yourself with a frozen face, forcing a mechanical smile; then watch as you turn your face down toward notes or a manuscript on a lectern. What effect do you think this facial behavior has in your efforts to communicate with an audience?

Now picture yourself stepping behind the same podium. This time you look out into the audience and smile warmly and naturally. Your face is natural and relaxed, as though you were talking with friends. Your eyes are directed out at the audience, for as Brown and Keller tell us: ". . . no feature of the face speaks so much for us as the eyes, poetically known as the windows of the soul."[12]

The term "eye contact" is somewhat superficial; there is more for the speaker's eyes to do than make contact with an audience, for this is often a mechanical sort of behavior. The eyes of the speaker should be looking into the audience for feedback. If communication is a reciprocal process—and it is—the speaker must seek feedback from the audience. If a speaker wants to communicate a genuine sense of interest, he or she will search the faces of the audience to let them known how important their feelings and reactions are.

In an intriguing essay, "Reflections on the Evil Eye," Richard Cass tells us "the eyes are a protective source of social stimulation and this may account for the intense fascination with the eyes by many cultural groups. The direction of a person's gaze is a powerful signal expressing interest in establishing contact or sustaining social interaction."[13]

It may be difficult to gaze directly at an audience in the process of making a speech. Looking into the eyes of another is not easy in many settings, especially when the other is a stranger. Think of getting on an elevator and riding for 60 to 120 seconds with a group of strangers. Does this group look directly at others? Probably not. Think of standing in front of an audience of strangers. Do you see yourself looking directly at these others? You should. Experiences in an elevator and public speaking settings are considerably different in many ways. When it comes to eye contact there is, however, an interesting similarity of avoidance of eye contact in many cases. A successful speaker needs to speak and to observe with his or her eyes in order to establish and maintain a direct relationship with the audience.

Crucial Behaviors for Communicators

Any kind of physical behavior, no matter how correct it may seem, can prove tiring to an audience if it is unvaried. A speaker needs to provide meaningful *activity* when appearing before an audience.

This general principle applies to the posture of speakers and is applicable to their specific gestural behavior. *A gesture is any movement of any part of the body that conveys some emotion or idea or reinforces words.* While movement generally involves changes in the location of the speaker, gesture consists of visible signs made with the hands, arms, head, face, and eyes. Good gestures, like good posture, do not draw attention to themselves and away from the ideas being communicated. They expand the ideas to be visualized and conceptualized by an audience. It is normal for an individual to gesture while speaking. Such behavior should be natural, appropriate, and consistent both with the ideas in the message and with the personality of the speaker.

We could suggest, as many texts do, specific gestures to be used in the presentation of a speech. This advice carries over from the eighteenth-century Elocutionary Movement. But the majority of students in a basic course who plan their gestures in detail look very mechanical when they speak. We can and should move and gesture in a *natural* way while attempting to be in control of ourselves as well. Remember that nonverbal elements in speaking often communicate to an audience in ways a speaker may not realize. For example, hands clasped tightly and nervously behind a speaker's back suggest discontent and tension. Eyes pointed toward the floor instead of at the audience indicate a lack of self-confidence.

Movement. The attention of an audience naturally follows and focuses on the speaker's movements. But movement, in order to enhance the meaning intended by a speaker, must be natural, easy, and purposeful, as we have said. Unless this is the case, the speaker distracts the audience and communicates anxiety and other feelings inconsistent with speaker's message.

One evening an instructor in speech communication was asked to serve as a substitute for the part-time teacher of an evening speech class at a community college. As the visiting instructor listened and watched the speakers in the class he became frustrated. The first two speakers wandered about the front of the room, talking all the while. When he criticized this behavior, the instructor found that the students had been told to move while talking—bad advice for them to follow. Movement should be used to complement ideas expressed verbally. A good way to use movement is when a speaker takes several steps while making a verbal transition; the physical movement corresponds with movement from one idea in the speech to another.

Movement provides a way to relieve physical tension, and so we should not hestitate to move as we speak. In fact, in a practice session if we extend our arms full length and turn completely around, we can identify a "speaking space" for movement. We are not limited to this space, but it can provide a comfortable area within which to move. If a speaker is small in stature, it is especially important to move out from the lectern so that the audience can see him or her.

If a lectern is to be used, movement also reminds a speaker that it is an aid and not a crutch. The lectern holds notes, not speakers. Often a speaker clutches or leans on the lectern throughout a presentation. This is distracting behavior and should be avoided. Speakers should stand back from the lectern.

The Arms and Hands. Inexperienced public speakers often feel uncertainty about what to do with their arms while speaking. One student reported quite honestly that his arms and hands felt like sides of beef hanging from his shoulders when he was about to make a speech. Gestures with the arms and hands should be easy, natural, and purposeful. Conventional gestures of the arms and hand which have meanings assigned to them by custom may be used. Clenching a fist, for example, indicates that the speaker feels strongly about a point being made. When the captured crew of the *Pueblo* was pictured by the North Koreans in 1968 for the "free world" to view, the photograph was supposed to illustrate a contented group of captives. But several men in the picture had their middle fingers extended in an obscene gesture known to millions of people in the United States and around the world. Theirs was a conventional gesture.

A descriptive gesture, on the other hand, generates meaning through depiction. When Joanne Little was on trial for killing a jail guard who, she claimed, had forced her sexually, she used descriptive gestures on the witness stand to help convey what she did and how she felt during the entire experience. Control of the arms and hands is important to projection and the achievement of the desired response from an audience. It is wise not to engage in mechanical or robotlike gestures, but one should not appear to be frozen with no gestures.

Nonverbal communication in public speaking should enhance the speaker's effort to achieve desired audience response. A number of distracting behaviors are identified later in this section of our study. It is crucial for the speaker seeking maximum effectiveness to understand that there is movement and gestural behavior which can definitely hamper successful communication. *Any movement, posture, or gesture which draws attention to itself and away from the intended meaning of the speech is a distraction and ought to be avoided.*

Speakers' Dress

If we watch a television talk show for a week and note the way the host, musicians, announcer, and guests are dressed, we find that each person is seeking to communicate something about himself or herself through dress. For example, Johnny Carson usually appears in a high-fashion outfit while his guests appear in a wide array of clothes. One unconventional and rebellious actor always wears a sweatshirt and blue jeans.

The college and university classrooms where public speaking is taught do not present the variety of styles that a television show does. But on campus we do seek to convey how we feel about ourselves, our life styles, and our attitudes toward the campus environment through our apparel.

A person who is about to make an important speech ought to consider his or her appearance carefully so that it is consistent with the purpose for speaking. A person's clothes should not be a barrier to communication. Remember: "Although we are not able at this time to specify the exact influence of each aspect of one's physical appearance in any given social situation, it seems fair to conclude that they may profoundly be important in some situations."[14]

Nonverbal Distractions

Students of public speaking should be concerned with movement and gestures in order to *eliminate* distractions. Here is a list of the ten most frequently occurring nonverbal distractions which bother audiences:

1. Nervous pacing
2. Frozen posture with no movement
3. Leaning on the lectern
4. Hands and arms locked tightly in front of or behind the body

 5. Scratching (oneself, the lectern)
 6. Rubbing hands, twisting rings or other jewelry
 7. Gesturing with a pen or pencil
 8. Covering mouth with a hand
 9. Jingling objects in pockets
10. Looking down or away from the audience.

Some might decide that this list is of minor concern to public speakers. But if we have a carefully developed speech, these distracting nonverbal behaviors are cheating both the speaker and the audience. Part of the message will not be processed in the minds of an audience which is annoyed and distracted by some physical movements of the speaker.

The Voice and How To Use It

Vocal production is somewhat of a miracle. The operation of the voice involves organs which have major functions other than the production of sound. For example, a speaker uses muscles and bones which have the major responsibility for respiration, mastication, and swallowing. Vocal folds protect the lungs from irritants in the atmosphere and help regulate the air flow. Knowing how sounds are produced provides public speakers with an appreciation of human vocal ability and with insight into how the voice can be fully used.

The organs of speech can be considered in two major categories: voice-producing, and articulating. The voice-producing mechanism includes the motor, the vibrator, and the resonators. The articulatory mechanism includes the tongue, teeth, lips, jaw, and the hard and soft palates. Speakers must use these organs to create sounds which are pleasant, appropriate, sharp, and interesting for an audience.

The breathing apparatus serves as the motor and as an energy source for voice production. This mechanism brings oxygen into the lungs as a source of fuel for the body and expels waste material. A speaker experiencing a particularly heavy emotional load due to performance anxiety will also have a heavier inhalation-exhalation cycle and may even hyperventilate—causing an abnormal loss of carbon dioxide from the blood. A speaker must breath deeply and naturally.

The vibrator consists of the vocal cords within the larynx, which is located at the upper end of the trachea and is connected above and below by muscles which move it up and down. Air compressed in the lungs during exhalation is processed through the trachea into the larynx. When sound is produced, the vocal cords come together until there is only a small slit between them. The air which is forced up the trachea and through the vocal cords in the larynx causes the cords to vibrate and to produce sounds. Speakers should breathe from their diaphragms to bring air up forcefully and produce clear and suitable volume. The diaphragm is located between the chest and abdomen and is the muscle wall which separates these two parts of the body.

The weak sound produced in the larynx by vibration of the vocal cords is expanded or resonated by a group of air chambers in the throat. The principal resonators of the voice are the upper part of the larynx, the throat, the nasal cavities, and the mouth. They amplify and modify sound, thus affecting vocal quality. Changes in the size and shape of some of these chambers result in different tones which constitute the vowel sounds. As the mouth is opened and closed, the size and shape of the oral cavity is changed, and the sound changes as well. Because the tonal quality of a voice is determined by the individual characteristics of the resonators, people can be recognized by the sound of their voices. Vocal quality in speakers is crucial to gaining and retaining the interest of an audience. Resonators can be used effectively by opening the mouth wide but without exaggeration as sound is amplified and modified.

The resonated sound is articulated into speech as the tongue, teeth, lips, jaw, and the hard and soft palates modify the production of speech sounds. By moving these articulators precisely, the size and shape of the mouth can be modified and the quality of tone can be controlled. The consonant interruptions in the flow of vowel sounds make words out of what otherwise would be merely vocal tones. Precision and sharpness of articulation come from the proper use of these modifiers. Lazy vocal habits will result in faulty enunciation. A speaker's task is to be precise, sharp, natural, and forceful in vocal production, while avoiding lazy and restrictive vocal habits.

Every member of an audience must be able to hear the speaker. Moreover, the speaker must learn to eliminate unnecessary pauses, and to convey meaning through *appealing vocal quality*. This is neither monotonous, harsh, nor shrill. Sound can be a powerful force in speaking. Change, variety, color, and interest in the voice help to convey meaning.

Volume, pitch, rate, pronunciation, and pauses are the elements of vocal delivery of most concern to public speakers. The speaker who shouts at an audience, chants at a level which strains the voice, speaks so rapidly that ideas are missed, runs words together, and pauses after every phrase or sentence is difficult to understand and probably creates little, if any, effect.

Volume. A speaker pushes sound out and produces volume by bringing the air for sound production from the diaphragm. Proper breathing provides volume, force, and control without strain. Most failures in vocal power are a result of weak volume, monotone, or overloudness. A speaker should speak out, but adjust the volume to a level appropriate to the rhetorical situation.

Volume must be suited to the physical setting of the public speaking occasion and the proximity of the speaker to the audience. In order to be heard, each speaker must work out a sufficient volume. For example, one lecturer used a large lecture hall with a speaker's stand in the center of the stage, a microphone mounted on the stand, and blackboards located to the right and out of range. The lecturer spoke in a normal tone of voice when using the microphone, but when he moved to the blackboards he increased volume through diaphragmatical breathing. It was as easy for the audience to hear him away from the microphone as it was before it.

A group of young people preparing a Christmas reading could not raise their volume so as to be heard in the room where the program was to be given. As a result, the audience had to watch seven young men and women read a Christmas story which few could hear.

Pitch. Pitch is a level of sound which depends upon the frequency of vibration of the vocal folds. That is determined by their length, thickness, and tension. A speaker raises or lowers the frequency of vibration depending on depth of thought and emotion.

Poor control of pitch results in a monotonous and chantlike effect. A speaker should operate within a range of pitch that is comfortable, normal, and pleasing. Variety and flexibility will keep pitch from contributing to vocal monotony.

Studies dealing with pitch suggest that a lively, flexible pitch pattern is not necessarily better for listening comprehension than speaking in a single pitch, but a falling pitch can create monotonous speaking and will decrease intelligibility for the audience.[15] An effective speaker can vary inflection to add to meaning.

An intercollegiate debater believed he should chant his affirmative speeches at a high shrill rather than in his normal conversational manner. After two tournaments and a number of judges' ballots, he realized what was hurting his chances for victory—the judges could hardly endure listening to him.

Rate. Speaking rate is a major problem with students presenting speeches in class. Many speak at so rapid a rate that few in the audience can follow, let alone remember, what is being said. By contrast, others speak so slowly that the audience becomes restless in anticipation of the conclusion.

The speaking rate should be appropriate to the ideas being expressed, to the flexibility of the speaker's vocal delivery, and to the speech setting. For example, describing a boxing match and describing a golf match call for two distinctly different vocal rates. In either event, the speaker must exercise control.

Two speech students demonstrating opposite extremes of speaking rate had trouble maintaining the attention of the audience. The first, speaking slowly and lazily, caused the audience to squirm, doodle, and shift their eyes about the room—all indications they were having trouble listening. The other spoke so rapidly that she sounded like a machine gun. The frustrated audience told her she must slow down if she wanted people to understand her.

Though it is not necessary to count words per minute, we can learn a desirable rate of speech or devise ways to become aware of our usual rates and improve on them. Studies indicate that comprehension by the audience is not affected significantly by rates varying from 120 to 160 words per minute, but the ease of listening decreases as rate increases. Slower rates appear to be most spontaneous and natural. Evidence does not prove that a rapid rate makes a speaker seem more dynamic and animated.[16]

Pause. Knowing when to pause is important to speech delivery. Some speakers will talk without taking a breath until they absolutely have to. Others make pauses after every three or four words and their delivery sounds choppy. Still others, particularly those who depend on a manuscript, pause at the wrong time—perhaps in the middle of an important idea—and disrupt the train of thought.

A fluent speaker allows ideas to unfold in a natural way, pausing appropriately and for lengths of time necessary for particular ideas to be conveyed. A master of the pause in message presentation is ABC news commentator Paul Harvey.

Research confirms that the rate of speech is determined by pauses within sentences and phrases.[17] The more appropriate the pause and the less obvious it appears, the more likely the speaker is to seem naturally fluent. The quality of communication suffers when a speaker relies heavily on the vocal pause—ahhhs and uuumms. Studies indicate that unfilled pauses made for the sake of clarity, emphasis, or rate variation can be effective; but that high levels of nonfluency impair delivery.[18]

A slow speaker who also pauses frequently adds to his or her monotony as a speaker. By contrast, a rapid speaker who does not pause at all except for "breath-catching" does not allow time for ideas to sink into the consciousness of the audience.

Pronunciation. In order to be understood, words must be expressed clearly and sharply. A presidential candidate from the East knew this and, when campaigning in the South, carefully changed his pronunciation of certain words and phrases in order to help him achieve identification with his Southern audiences.

It would be incorrect for us to prescribe a particular standard for pronunciation, because regional and cultural dialects vary throughout the country. Which is most appropriate? All of them. A speaker should use his or her regional and cultural standard in an articulate way so audiences can hear and understand every word. A guide to pronunciation is given in any good dictionary. A speaker bent on improving pronunciation should be familiar with the language to be used, attack words sharply, pause appropriately, and avoid running words and phrases together in a sloppy, speedy, or lazy fashion.

Studies suggest no significant difference in comprehension when varying levels of mispronunciation have been used. If the mispronunciation is considerable, however, listening becomes difficult for many auditors. Audiences who are aware of proper pronunciation react with diminishing credibility to the speaker whose speech does not sound intelligent because of mispronunciation.[19] Good pronunciation is an important ingredient in effective public communication. A wealthy industrialist was speaking before a college audience on one occasion, and because he had had a minimal education in communication skills, he frequently mispronounced or poorly pronounced many of his words. The audience of parents, students, faculty, and administrators, though grateful for his financial support of the college, were embarrassed by him as a speaker.

The Ethos of the Speaker

Speakers must be favorably received by audiences, and they must be thought of as honest and truthful. This need can be filled by the strong ethos, or moral stance, of a speaker, and by the ethical responsibility projected. The audience's perception of a speaker as a person to believe or ignore has long been one of the most significant factors in determining his or her effectiveness. Aristotle spoke of ethos, or ethical appeal, as one of three modes of persuasion a speaker could employ to influence the behavior of an audience. *Ethos is the perceived "goodness" of the speaker by the audience.* It is acquired in a variety of ways before an audience hears a speech. There can be additional impressions of "goodness" gained for the speaker during the delivery of the speech.

What factors compose ethos? Aristotle described three: *intelli-*

gence, sagacity, good will. This means that if a speaker convinces an audience he or she is an intelligent person, who possesses wisdom, and who has good intentions, particularly toward the audience, the audience will be influenced by the speaker.[20] Current research has expanded these three elements of ethos by studying what researchers label *speaker credibility.* For example, behavioral scientists indicate that credibility depends on two factors: competence or expertness accorded to the source of a message by the receivers; and trust-worthiness ascribed to the speaker by the audience.[21] These factors are behind the familiar cliche of a political figure who flashes a gruesome-looking picture of an opponent to viewing audiences while asking: "Would you buy a used car from this man?" The implication is that a man who looks like that is neither expert nor trustworthy.

Other researchers have added safety, qualifications, and dynamism to the dimensions of credibility. In summarizing this research Ervin P. Bettinghaus has noted that safety refers to the speaker being perceived as "kind, congenial, friendly, agreeable, pleasant, gentle, unselfish, just, forgiving, fair, hospitable, warm, cheerful, sociable, ethical, calm, and patient."[22] A speaker perceived of as highly quali-fied is thought to be "trained, experienced, qualified, skilled, in-formed, authoritative, able, and intelligent." Dynamism refers to a speaker's appearance.

Other factors have emerged as being important to credibility. Personal, professional, or social status can give a spokesperson credibility in the eyes of an audience. Credibility is also helpful or hindered, at times, by the expressed views of opinion leaders.

Followers of Oral Roberts—Christian, healer, preacher, author, and educator—believe him to possess extremely high ethos and credibility as a public speaker because he is perceived as being a man of character, good will, and intelligence. To this audience Roberts possesses competence and truthworthiness, as well as the dimensions of safety, qualifications, and dynamism. Others, for whom Roberts has low ethos and credibility, would argue that he does not possess these factors.

Ethos and *credibility* are crucial to a speaker's effect on an audience. Bound into the factors of ethos and credibility are the *ethics* of public speech communication.

Ethos and Ethics

A major contention of this book is that *ethics* plays a crucial role in the stance of the speaker and in the response of the audience to the speaker and the speech. Ethics is a subject of major importance to any thoughtful student of speech. Consider these statements, for instance:

1. If the U.S. Air Force began bombing attacks on a small nation and told the citizens that these were not bombing raids but protective-reaction strikes, how would you feel?
2. If you were not a Moslem, how would you feel if an adherent of Islam told you without question that Allah is the true God and Mohammed is his prophet?
3. If you heard a noted elected official publicly praise a famous business woman for her contribution to the community, and then you heard this same official privately tell the businesswoman that if she wanted to maintain her business she had to pay the official $100,000 annually, how would you feel?
4. If a professor in a large lecture session admitted to the class that she realized only about 5 percent of the students could understand her but that was "okay" because she was only concerned with this particular 5 percent, how would you feel?

The answers to these and similar questions are at the foundation of ethics in human communication, for when one speaks and another listens the choice of ideas is one involving ethics. Whether a speaker's motives lie hidden or are at the surface of the mind, the feelings and information that emerge are related to a set of values. They identify the standards of conduct which are a part of an individual system of values, learned as a set of rules for making choices. *The rules are ethics.* Ethical implications are clearly evident when one speaks in public and others respond. Ethical standards are essential in determining one's behavior as a communicator.

A useful approach to viewing ethics in public speaking is to consider speakers in terms of whether they are dialogic or monologic with an audience. Dialogue and monologue, in this sense, are not formats or techniques for speaking but rather are ethical orientations and attitudes toward achieving effectiveness with an audience. Richard Johannesen has probably explained dialogue and monologue best when he writes:

> Dialogic communication is usually viewed as ethical and monologic communication as unethical. Dialogue is held to be more fully human, humane, and facilitative of personal self-fulfillment than is monologue. Dialogue and monologue represent more of a communication attitude or orientation than a specific method, technique, or format. We speak of dialogue or monologue as permeating a given human communication transaction. . . . In monologue the attitude of senders toward receivers is marked by such qualities as deception, superiority, exploitation, dogmatism, domination, insincerity, pretense, personal display, self-aggrandizement, coercion, distrust, self-defensiveness, and viewing the Other as an object to be manipulated. The speaker views receivers as objects to be exploited for self-serving purposes; they are not taken seriously as persons. Focus is on the speaker's message, not on the audience's real needs. The core values, goals and policies espoused by the speaker are impervious to influence exerted by receivers. Audience feedback is used only to further the speaker's purpose; an honest response from receivers is not wanted or is precluded. Often choices are narrowed and consequences obscured. . . . Dialogue, in contrast, is characterized by such attitudes as honesty, concern for the welfare of the Other, trust, genuineness, openmindedness, equality, mutual respect, empathy, directness, lack of pretense, nonmanipulative intent, encouragement of free expression, and acceptance of the Other as a unique individual regardless of differences over belief or behavior. Although the speaker in dialogue may offer advice or express disagreement, he does not aim to psychologically coerce an audience into accepting his view. The speaker's aim is one of assisting the audience in making independent, self-determined decisions. While the speaker expresses judgment of

policies and behaviors, judgment of the intrinsic worth of audience members is avoided.[23]

Dialogue and monologue are an attitude, orientation, principle, or spirit rather than a method, procedure, or technique. In terms of ethics, as we define it here, the dialogic communicator operates from a view of the audience which seems ethical, while the monological communicator appears the opposite. Dialogue in speaking and listening has been characterized by such attitudes as honesty, empathy, directness with lack of pretense, nonmanipulative intent, and encouragement of free expression, as well as respect for and acceptance of the other person as a unique individual, regardless of differences over beliefs or behavior.

The monologic speaker employs devices such as deception, superiority, exploitation, dogmatism, domination, insincerity, pretense, personal self-display, self-aggrandizement, coercion, distrust, self-defensiveness, and viewing the other as an object to be manipulated. In this view speakers view audiences as objects, not persons, to be manipulated for self-serving purposes; the audience is not taken seriously.

Each person possesses a system of values which provide rules for making judgments about what is to be perceived as "the good" and "the bad." This system is deep-seated and guides behavior. Though values, once established, remain relatively constant in a person, they can and do change in the process of living.

The study of ethics in public speaking can increase self-understanding and enhance meaningful communication between the self and the audience. General guidelines about ethics in public-speech communication should be kept in mind. Perhaps of particular importance are these:

1. Ethos and credibility are crucial in communication. If you are the speaker be aware of your ethos and credibility and what they mean to your person and purpose as a communicator; if you are in the audience be aware of the part ethos and credibility play in your response to what you hear and to whom.
2. Ethical systems and the necessity for making decisions often

lead to some sort of moral judgment by speakers and audiences. Ethics is a crucial factor in deciding between what is perceived to be "right" and "wrong" or "valuable" and "not valuable." Understand the nature of your ethical system, and try to perceive those of others when you are the speaker.

In an introduction to public speaking, ethical responsibility is usefully explained in two ways. First, the highest ethical obligation in public speech communication is a commitment to full and effective expression of opinions, information-sharing, and decision-maknig. Second, the speaker must have a commitment to express views consistent with his or her personal value system—what one really believes at each point in life to be true and accurate. As a speaker each of us has the responsibility of communicating without violating our personal knowledge and values. As a communicator each of us can be willing to provide for full expression, as well as for free expression. Situations may arise in which a speaker must serve as a spokesperson for a point of view not his or her own (in the commitment to full expression), but this can be done in a way consistent with ethical responsibility. "The events of our time and those in recent years especially point to the need for some attempt to define the limits and responsibilities of speakers in our form of society. Change will always present men and women with struggle for progressive achievements, and for the good life. Speech communication will be essential in any human struggle significant to the quality of human life, so there will continue to be a need to define, establish, and maintain ethical responsibility."[24]

SUMMARY

The four basic needs of speakers were examined. The first two centered on speech tension and how to deal with it. Though unsettling to many speakers, speech tension is a normal state of anxiety occurring in anyone confronted with a speaking situation in which the performance is important and the outcome is uncertain. Its symptoms are generally three: physiological, negative self-evaluation, and withdrawal. The causes are four: desire to be successful in speaking, an approach/avoidance conflict within the self, a feeling of inadequacy, and a distortion of the speech situation. At the heart of each cause is self-consciousness and a preoccupation with one's own discomfort. The key to control is to become message- and audience-centered rather than self-centered, and to remember that audiences usually are made up of friendly people. Careful preparation and speaking experience can serve to reduce nervousness.

Speakers must use their bodies and voices as effectively as possible. Being dull to hear and watch is tedious, frustrating, and boring for any audience. Delivery is important nonverbal communication. Often speakers do not realize the inconsistency between their intended messages and their physical projections. Facial expressions and observation for feedback by the speaker serve to assist in establishing a direct relationship between speaker and audience, movement, gestures, and posture play a significant part in establishing this relationship. These convey ideas and emotions just as words do. They can also detract from the speaker's meaning, and distractions ought to be avoided. The ten most frequent distractions were cited.

The voice should be used with maximum effectiveness. Understanding vocal mechanisms is important in that effort. The five most important elements of vocal delivery are volume, pitch, rate, pronunciation, and pausing.

Ethos is a major concern of communication theorists. People are likely to be influenced by the spokesperson they view as being intelligent, trustworthy, and dynamic, and as having good will, integrity, authoritativeness, and competence. It may be difficult for one speaker to possess all these attributes, but anyone, through effort, can heighten his or her ethos and credibility with an andience.

It is natural to discuss ethics in public communication, for ethics play a crucial role in one's role as a speaker, as well as in the audience's response to the speaker and the speech. The ethical speaker can be described as dialogic, while the monologic speaker appears as unethical. Dialogue is an orientation characterized by honesty, empathy, lack of pretense, nonmanipulative intent; monologue is characterized as exploitation, deception, superiority, dogmatism, self-aggrandizement, coercion, and distrust. One can learn a great deal about oneself and an audience by viewing the role ethics plays in a speaker-audience relationship. It is to the audience specifically that we now turn.

NOTES

1. Raymond S. Ross, *Speech Communication: Fundamentals and Practice,* 2d ed. (Englewood Cliffs: Prentice-Hall, 1970), pp. 35–36.
2. Bent Bradley, *Speech Performance* (Dubuque: William C. Brown, 1968), pp. 30–44.
3. John J. Makay and Thomas C. Sawyer, *Speech Communication Now! An Introduction to Rhetorical Influences* (Columbus: Charles E. Merrill, 1973), pp. 33–40.
4. Mark Knapp, "The Field of Nonverbal Communication: An Overview," in *On Speech Communication,* ed. Charles J. Stewart (New York: Holt, Rinehart & Winston, 1972), p. 65.
5. Ibid., p. 65.
6. Makay and Sawyer, *Speech Communication Now!,* p. 166.
7. Professor Galloway is on the faculty in the College of Education at The Ohio State University. His research has been devoted to nonverbal communication. This information comes from the *Columbus Dispatch,* "Reality without Words," June 3, 1975.
8. Randall P. Harrison and Wayne W. Crouch, "Nonverbal Communication: Theory and Research," in *Communication and Behavior,* ed. Gerhard J. Hanneman and William J. McEwen (Reading: Addison-Wesley, 1975), pp. 76–97.
9. Makay and Sawyer, *Speech Communication Now!,* p. 165.
10. Albert Mehrabian, *Silent Messages* (Belmont: Wadsworth Publishing Co., 1971), p. 43.
11. Charles T. Brown and Paul W. Keller, *From Monologue to Dialogue: Exploration in Interpersonal Communication* (Englewood Cliffs: Prentice-Hall, 1973), p. 63.
12. Ibid., p. 63.
13. Richard G. Cass, "Reflections on the Evil Eye," *Human Behavior,* October 1974, pp. 16–22.
14. Mark Knapp, "The Field of Nonverbal Communication: An Overview," in *On Speech Communication,* ed. Charles J. Stewart (New York: Holt, Rinehart & Winston, 1972), p. 65.

15. Charles F. Diehl, Richard C. White, and Paul H. Statz, "Pitch Change and Comprehension," *Speech Monographs,* March 1961, pp. 65–68.
16. See Carole H. Hearst, "Listening Comprehension as a Function of Type of Material and Rate of Presentation," *Speech Monographs,* June 1968, pp. 154–58; Kenneth A. Harwood, "Listenability and Rate of Presentation," *Speech Monographs,* March 1955, pp. 27–59; and George Gunkle, "An Experimental Study of Some Vocal Characteristics of Spontaneity in Acting," *Speech Monographs,* June 1968, pp. 158–65.
17. See, for example, J.G. Angrello, "A Study of Intra and Inter Phrasal Pauses and Their Relationship to the Rate of Speech" (Ph.D. diss., The Ohio State University, 1963).
18. See, for example, the excellent summary in Richard C. Crable's essay, "A Situational Approach to Purposeful Nonverbal Communication," in *Exploration in Speech Communication,* ed. John J. Makay (Columbus: Charles E. Merrill, 1973), pp. 299–314.
19. David W. Addington, "The Effect of Mispronunciations on General Speaking Effectiveness," *Speech Monographs,* June 1965, pp. 159–163; Larry L. Barker, Robert J. Kibler, and Francis J. Kelley, "Effect of Perceived Mispronunciations on Speech Effectiveness Ratings and Retention," *Quarterly Journal of Speech,* February 1968, pp. 47–58.
20. *Aristotle's Rhetoric,* trans. Layne Cooper (New York: Appleton-Century-Crofts, 1960).
21. Ervin P. Bettinghaus, *Persuasive Communication,* 2d ed. (New York: Holt, Rinehart & Winston, 1973), p. 103.
22. Ibid., p. 103.
23. Richard L. Johannesen, "Attitude of the Speaker toward the Audience: A Significant Concept for Contemporary Rhetorical Theory and Criticism," *Central States Speech Journal,* Summer 1974, pp. 95–104.
24. Makay and Sawyer, *Speech Communication Now!.* See especially chap. 11, "Communication Ethics," pp. 217–39.

CHAPTER 3

UNDERSTANDING AUDIENCE BEHAVIOR

The success and effect of a public speaker are determined by the audience. As we have learned, communication is not for self-aggrandizement and display but to achieve a specific purpose with an audience. To do this it is necessary to concentrate on the four essential needs of an audience. Then the audience can be analyzed and can be brought around to the speaker's point of view.

To review, a speaker who wants to understand and relate to an audience realistically will have to—

1. understand how audiences process information;
2. know about the nature of attitudes, beliefs, and values within audiences;
3. know what essential questions must be answered for a practical audience analysis;

4. know about the basic types of audiences a public communicator will usually face.

When a speaker has information that satisfies these four needs, she or he can make a genuine effort to speak directly to audiences so that they can understand the speaker's message. The successful and effective speaker is audience-centered rather than self-centered. Knowledge about an audience is essential to good speech construction, which is discussed in chapter 4. This chapter, which is more theoretical than earlier ones, discusses concepts of audience behavior.

Analysis of an audience is an investigative process—the speaker is looking for knowledge and information about how audiences respond to public speakers and what important data should be obtained for a particular audience. Communication studies provide us with practical ways of focusing audience analysis. The speaker who shows no real awareness and understanding of a particular audience is likely to experience rhetorical failure. This sort of failure is evident when one considers the rational person versus the psychological person in facing an audience.

Rational versus Psychological Persons

Imagine for some moments a typical luncheon with a speaker set in a small town. It is a college town, and the occasion is a weekly meeting of a men's service club, which always features a guest speaker. The time is noon. About 110 men have arrived. The meal is starchy and is followed by ritual (singing of "My Country 'Tis of Thee," Pledge of Allegiance to the Flag, and a prayer offered by one of the local clergymen). Announcements from the organization's president are made. With about 40 minutes left for the meeting, the speaker for the day is introduced. On this particular occasion he is a teacher and researcher in health education, and his current interest is the hazards of smoking cigarettes. The audience is white and ranges in age from twenty-three to seventy, with the majority of the audience in their forties. They tend to be quite conservative in their economic, political, and regional attitudes, beliefs, and values.

The majority are college-educated and are businessmen. They seem pleasant and friendly.

The speaker is introduced by name and title only. He has not provided a specific title for his talk. The audience is told only that the message is to deal with smoking and health. The audience seems to be dominated by cigarette smokers, and there is a sprinkling of cigar and pipe smokers as well. (Remember that the specific purpose of any speech is the precise response a speaker wants from the audience.) As the audience listens, it becomes apparent that a significant problem for the speaker is that the specific purpose of the speech is largely unclear. The purpose of the speech seems different to different members of the audience; the speaker's message spreads over a wide pattern of lines of reasoning, perhaps with the expectation that some of his ideas might hit their mark.

There are also two general problems which are central to the two main areas of behavior in public speech communication—content and delivery. The content, or substance, of the message *is not well suited to the particular audience*, and the delivery is dull. The

speaker's tone is monotonous and lacks animation. There is no effort made to hold the attention of this audience, persons who have worked hard all morning and have just completed a heavy lunch. The content of the speech is a compact essay reporting scientific research on the hazards of smoking, and it is conveyed in highly technical language.

The audience is experiencing a poor reading of a lengthy manuscript by a speaker who obviously is not skilled in interpretive reading. He also does not have the security, ability, and common sense to speak from an outline in a conversational way. If only he could bring this message to life through language and expression! The speaker's task is to respond to the needs of the audience so they can respond to him in a way consistent with his intentions.

This speaker's communication with the audience can be identified as the "rational-person approach." The speaker did not use the "psychological-person approach," one which requires audience analysis and adaptation.

Consider the distinction between these two means of addressing an audience. The rational-person approach operates on the assumption that if the speaker musters all the facts and ideas that communicate clarity and truth for him or her, the audience will obviously understand and accept the speaker's message. It assumes that what is unquestionably logical and right for one person (the speaker) ought to be logical and right for anyone exposed to the same information (the audience), whether or not the psychological characteristics and make-up which affect the thoughts and actions of speaker and audience are the same. Far too often speakers operate on the assumption that "all I have to do is put together my message, and if the facts say something to me and my values are essential, no straight-thinking person can seriously question or challenge me." This was the assumption the speaker on smoking hazards used. He planned to travel about the region addressing a variety of audiences, reading the same speech without any modification or adjustment. He had a highly rational message—for him. But the audience had trouble listening.

Effective speaking requires the adjustment of information to an audience so that it can understand the information. In the rational-person approach to speaking this is not likely to happen.

If a speaker realistically wants to ensure that his audience can create a meaning similar to what was in his or her mind, a "psychological-person approach" should be used. In this manner of speaking a person looks into herself or himself, as well as *other sources*, for information for the speech. The speaker also understands how people process information, and investigates the audience to learn about its background and opinions. The speaker wants to know how the audience feels, thinks, and acts. All of these data are then related to the specific purpose of the speech. Because audiences differ both in terms of the individuality of each member and in their collective image, adjustments and modifications by the speaker influenced by the psychology of the audience become necessary.

A senior at a large university had been a major in engineering for 3 years when he suddenly decided to enter politics. He took some speaking courses to prepare himself for addressing political groups. One of the course assignments required that each student prepare and deliver a speech persuading an audience to a specific end. The day before he was to speak the senior read a highly philosophical essay about "the meaning of democracy" to his instructor. This was the persuasive speech the senior planned to read the next day, and he asked the instructor if he should do so. The instructor said two things—the content was not suited to the audience; his reading would not be an acceptable mode of delivery. The student became defensive and left muttering something about making some changes. The next day, he rattled the essay off from memory while the class—mostly freshmen new to the campus—restlessly waited for him to finish. Instead of a discussion and critique of the speech the instructor asked each person to comment on what the speech had meant. The comments clearly indicated that the speaker had failed to persuade anyone to his point of view. The audience was "turned off" by his abstract language and unnatural delivery. Most perceived the speaker as an upper classman who might be trying to impress them with his knowledge, but certainly was not trying to communicate with them. He did not use a psychological-person approach to this audience. He was largely self- and not audience-centered, and simply assumed his listeners would see, understand, and accept his ideas when they heard what he had to say. The psychological-person approach in public speaking would have guided the speaker to target his message to the specific wants, needs, and desires of the audience as they related to the speaker's specific purpose.

The goal of the public speaking course is to make students into speakers. It is good to be rational in the construction and presentation of a speech, but careful attention to audience behavior and a particular audience on each occasion is needed. None of us can peer into the mind of each listener. But speakers can do their utmost in a practical way to relate to listening behavior and to the behavior of an audience as a collective body.

To understand what often happens in the listening behavior of an audience, we turn now to the ideas of William R. Brown.[1]

Understanding Information Processing in Audiences

One unique and realistic way to learn about audience analysis is to understand a basic way in which audiences process the information they hear. We know from studies in human behavior that there are some relatively typical ways in which persons deal with speeches, depending on their feelings and ideas about a particular topic, subject, speaker, and occasion. A "filtering process" (recall the perception model in chapter 1) takes place during a speech so that certain portions of the message are left out by listeners while others are admitted and processed in listeners' thoughts. Studies tell us that the intentions of the speaker's message can be *bent* and *distorted* by an audience. In a sense listeners do not understand a speaker's meanings exactly in the same way as the speaker does. Three particular dimensions of listening behavior are explained by Brown. These illustrate the point that a speaker's effect depends to some extent on the information processing of the auditors. Brown introduces his readers to three inevitable ways listeners might treat a speaker's message:

1. assimilation-contrast
2. addition-deletion
3. rationalization

Let's consider each of these.[2]

Assimilation-Contrast. An audience is assimilating a speech when it sees similarities where differences also exist. This results in an audience's not understanding a speaker's view in the same way the speaker does. The differences may be ignored if listeners assimilate what they think a speaker is saying. But if the audience is processing information by pushing a speaker's views to extremes that were never intended, it can be said that listeners are *contrasting* the speech and making the speaker's views (in their interpretation) considerably different from the intended meaning.

Within each person are a limited number of personal and shared basic values which can be thought of as "inner self-anchors." Brown imagines these anchors as clusters centered in concerns for *survival, acceptance, new experience,* and *mastery.* For instance, we value our lives and those of others important to us; we want to accept certain ideas, experiences, and things that seem to us to make life worthwhile; we seek new experiences in order to grow and escape boredom; and we strive to master tasks for self-satisfaction and productive living.

Joseph, a student, may possess deep-seated self-anchors which help him to choose what food to eat; certain ideas that give him intellectual satisfaction; particular socializing experiences for adventuresome diversions from the rigors of course work; and ways to learn and complete assignments to achieve good grades in pursuit of a chosen profession. If Joseph listens to a speaker and acts in agreement with these particular values, we can say he becomes particularly ego-involved.

There is some *ambiguity* or vagueness in all messages from public speaking and from other forms of communication. This ambiguity exists in public speaking because language takes on meaning assigned by the speaker and by members of the audience. The meaning *can* be shared and similar, but it *cannot* be exactly the same. The speaker does not transplant one idea from his or her mind into the mind of another. Using language, both speaker and listener *create meaning* for themselves; exact and perfect communication is, therefore, not possible.

Just as ambiguity of language affects the intended message of a speaker, both ambiguity of language and these intentions to some degree affect the interpretation of a listener with respect to the ego involvement of that listener. The more the audience experiences strong or positive ego-involvement and similar values with the speaker, the more the audience will be likely to agree with the speaker. This is called *assimilation*. On the contrary, the less the intentions of the speaker, as shown by his or her language, match those of the audience, and the less ego involvement the audience experiences, the more likely it is that *contrasting* will occur. A wise public speaker recognizes that an audience will distort intended meaning through assimilation and contrast. *The speaker will seek to empathize with each audience on the basis of audience analysis, and will carefully try to increase the likelihood of shared meaning between speaker and audience.*

Ego involvement and values are clearly important in producing additions and deletions as audiences perceive speeches, and these also affect assimilation and contrast.

Addition-Deletion. Listeners will frequently add and delete information included in a speech. Addition and deletion is likely to continue in the minds of an audience when persons think about what they saw and heard and when they tell others about a speech. A number of reasons may explain this occurrence. Listeners may feel there is inconsistency between what a speaker says and what values and information they hold, so the listeners simply overlook information they *do not want to hear,* and *embellish ideas and facts that are desirable and consistent with their value systems.*

If a listener is a political conservative and hears a conservative speaker advocate a liberal view, that auditor may delete the liberal ideas and add conservative statements in his or her own mind. Auditors have a rich store of information and understanding about some topics, and sparse information and understanding about others. If they are knowledgeable, and perhaps favorable toward a speaker's subject, they will add meanings. If their information, understanding, and interest is slight, auditors are likely to delete portions of the speech. For example, a university student majoring in drama and taking required science courses in order to complete a bachelor's degree, will have no trouble adding to drama lectures, but must struggle to keep from deleting information at a botany lecture.

The speaker must understand the audience's probable storehouse of information. Distortion caused by addition and deletion should be minimized as much as possible.

Rationalization. Because all of us seek to be comfortable with ourselves, with others, and with the world, we find ourselves *rationalizing* in order to establish a comfortable self and to justify human behavior. As members of an audience we frequently respond to a speaker and a speech with images centered in ourselves. This requires us to think about the image in order to reach a comfortable state. The process of intellectualizing strives for inner consistency, or mental and emotional balance, so that we feel reasonably settled about our conclusions or can gain peace of mind and body. People seem to have a tremendous capacity for rationalizing human behavior and natural events. Rationalizing is logical and sound if the symbolic reality takes actuality into account. The speaker should remember that people learn to deal with the inconsistencies of their lives, in part, through rationalization.

If we accept the notion that human beings strive for a balanced existence and want to feel physically and psychologically comfortable, *we can predict some of their reactions to our intentions as speakers*. Many want to be intellectually and spiritually in tune with themselves and their views of the world. The many physicians, psychologists, educators, and spiritual leaders in our society are evidence enough that humans strive for personal balance and ways to deal effectively with life. There seems to be continual search for homeostasis—balance—both in body and personality. A primary way to achieve homeostasis can be through rationalization helping us to adjust to our own states and our interactions with others. But because of the tendency to assimilate and contrast, to add and delete, rationalization can also contribute to message ambiguity, bending, and distorting.

The spokesperson who has a *sound and thorough understanding of the audience—and who can shape a message to minimize ambiguity, bending, and distortion—is most likely to achieve the specific purpose for making a speech*. This point is crucial for effective public speaking. To increase the likelihood of gaining a sound and thorough understanding of the audience, we must focus on listeners' attitudes, beliefs, and values which influence how they will perceive information. We cannot peer into each listener's mind before we speak, but we can have a clear idea of the psychological constructs in human behavior and try to plan and predict how an audience will receive our message.

The Psychology of the Audience

The psychological dimensions we know as attitudes, beliefs, and values are central to our opinions. An audience is made up of individuals who possess a multitude of attitudes, beliefs and basic values, which influence their reception of a speech through assimilation-contrast, addition-deletion, rationalization, and the knowledge they have acquired. This involves hearing, selecting, comprehending, interpreting, evaluating, and deciding about the speech. To be fully audience-centered, speakers must have a basic understanding of the nature of these psychological features and their importance to the public speaker.

Attitudes. "What is an attitude?" Many researchers in the social and behavioral sciences devote entire careers to dealing with this question and others related to it. A satisfactory answer for the student of communication is that an attitude is a "mental and neural state of readiness, organized through experience, exerting a direc- tive or dynamic influence upon the individual's response to all objects and situations with which it is related."[2]

Perhaps the chief characteristics of attitudes are:

1. to be aimed at an object, situation, event, issue, or person;
2. to be characterized by direction, degree, and intensity;
3. to be a learned response;
4. to be generally stable and enduring.

We can also say that an attitude consists of three fundamental di- mensions: (1) cognitive, (2) affective, (3) behavioral. The cognitive dimension consists of the knowledge and beliefs we have about an object, situation, event, issue, or person. Our feelings are bound into the affective dimension; they are our emotions. Action influ- ences the behavioral dimension of an attitude.

Sharon, a housewife in her early thirties, belonged to a women's organization in her community. One evening she attended a special program sponsored by the organization which featured a speech by a local funeral director, "Death, Grief, and the Funeral Director." Sharon's attitudes toward the speaker, his profession, and the topic were quite negative. Her attitudes toward the women's organization and their special programs was quite favorable. Sharon did not want to have any dealings with funeral directors unless she had to. She had read and believed in several books critical of "the funeral business," and had heard stories which reinforced this negative criticism. She had only attended two funerals in her life, and regarded them as somewhat "spooky," unfortunate dramatic shows produced and directed by persons in the funeral business. Sharon's attitudes about death and grief were mixed. Her religious background stressed death as an extension of life to those "in a state of grace." The stability of this attitude was undergoing discomforting changes because of information that was weakening her religious faith. Grief and death were matters of limited experience for her, and she tried not to think about them. She had some personal fear about death because it was unknown.

In Sharon's attitude about funeral directors there is inner direction for disassociation with the profession—a highly unfavorable predisposition toward them. Her intensity of feeling was hostile. These factors created a strong feeling of dislike toward the speaker and his topic, and they made her tend to avoid the program. Yet, she associated very strongly with the event and persons sponsoring the evening. She was favorably predisposed toward her peers in the organization, and she felt intensely committed to supporting its programs. These factors were also shaped by her knowledge, beliefs, and what she liked. Her positive attitude resulted in her going to this particular program. Sharon's generally stable attitudes toward the women's organization and toward the funeral business would certainly affect her hearing of the speaker and her reaction to his message.

The speaker is often faced with an audience of individuals with attitudes similar to Sharon's. Mark, the funeral director who spoke, had a general notion that there would be mixed attitudes about him, who and what he represented, and his topic. After determining the precise response he wanted from his audience, he conducted an analysis so that he could take an audience-centered approach to this speaking engagement. Trying to uncover prevailing attitudes within the audience is a practical way of beginning an audience analysis. A further step includes learning about core values within an audience.

Beliefs. Consider belief as a degree of faith and acceptance interrelated with an attitude and a value. One may believe (have faith in and/or accept) that the president of the United States is honest; one universal God does exist; the sun will come up tomorrow. One may also accept quite the opposite: the president is not honest; there is no universal God; and the sun will not come up tomorrow. Milton Rokeach has written exhaustively on the subject of beliefs.[3] He defines belief as "a simple proposition, conscious or unconscious, capable of being preceded by the phrase 'I believe that . . .'" Rokeach describes three types of beliefs: *existential*, those capable being true or false; *evaluative*, those where the objective of belief is judged to be good or bad; and *proscriptive*, those where the end of action is judged to be desirable or undesirable. Rokeach argues that beliefs and values, have cognitive, affective, and behavioral components just as attitudes do.

A centrality-peripherality model of beliefs is offered by Rokeach. In this model he distinguishes between five general classes of belief, with the first being most central and the fifth most peripheral for a person. Let us look closely at this model.

1. *Primitive belief #1.* Those learned through direct experience by a person with an object, and which are supported by social consensus
2. *Primitive belief #2.* Those which do not depend on social consensus but rather on deep personal experience
3. *Authority belief.* Those in which who or what to trust or not to trust is supported by negative or positive authority
4. *Belief derived from authorities.* Those positions assimilated from sources with which an individual identifies
5. *Inconsequential belief.* Those which direct behavior but are not highly significant when compared with others

Theoretically, primitive beliefs are seldom changed by communication. Authoritative beliefs can be changed through communication; While inconsequential beliefs are perhaps most easy to change. To understand the theory reasonably well each of us should make a list of our beliefs on some subjects divided by these categories.

Jane, an executive with the state department of mental health and retardation, holds a primitive belief in total abstinence from alcoholic beverages. It is based on her experiences with her alcoholic father and is supported by tenets of the Morman faith she has held since her conversion several years ago. Tom is a pacifist and has suffered from harrassment ever since he first sought conscientious-objector status during the Vietnam War. Sara believed without much question that electrical-rate hikes were always necessary because her husband, a director of consumer relations at the electric company, told her this was so. He offered little explanation as to why; it was simply that for her he was a positive authority whom she trusted about this issue. Ben, an employee working for Sara's husband, shared this belief but his depended on the authoritative sources he encountered during his daily work. Bunny believed that the language used in R-rated movies is often profane and obscene. But in contrast with beliefs in which she is genuinely ego-involved, this belief is rather inconsequential and weak. Jane, Tom, Sara, Ben, and Bunny have a number of beliefs which range from central primitive to peripheral inconsequential beliefs—as we all do. *When we speak to an audience, or are spoken to as members of an audience, the effect of the speaker's message is influenced by the way the speaker's ideas are interpreted by the audience in relation to the beliefs held by members of that audience. Analyzing the audience calls for as much knowledge as possible about the patterns of belief shared by members of the audience about the speaker, the purpose, and the occasion for speaking.*

For instance, a speaker who knows the general objective and specific purpose of a speech would investigate the psychology of the audience to try to discover *prevailing beliefs* and *patterns of belief* which are crucial to the way in which the audience would process the speaker's information. Betty recently gave a speech in which she hoped to persuade her audience to lift a ban on courses in human sexuality in their community school system. Betty failed to take into account the overwhelming pattern of primitive belief in this audience, which can best be described as "detailed discussions of sex are the parents' responsibility." She did not focus carefully on working with this pattern of belief. Her audience listened politely and was not moved in the least. Indeed, persuading the audience might involve a carefully planned series of speeches without guarantee of success. But if Betty genuinely wanted to be effective, she would have had to understand audience behavior. Learning about beliefs in the audience is essential to the public speaker. At the core of attitudes and beliefs are values, so a thorough audience analyst also needs to discover some basic information about values.

Values. Deep within each person is a cluster of values, perhaps only between 12 and 20, which makes up a value system. Attitudes and beliefs are grounded in values, as we have seen in our discussions of ethos and information-processing. Values are at the very core of audience behavior, but they are often difficult to define. *A value can be a deep-seated standard or central psychological anchor which serves as the basis for ethical guidance and approach/avoidance behavior.*

Beatrice Nugent attempted to identify dominant American values.[4] Her review of completed research is significant for the public speaker. A speaker may be effective or ineffective with an audience because of her or his appeal or lack of it to values held by the audience. In her research Nugent hypothesized that a successful public communicator appealed to values shared by the audience. Her research, a case study, confirmed this hypothesis.

Of particular interest to public speaking are the descriptions of values, the value system, and the value postulates Nugent uncovered. Because audiences to a large extent behave according to their values, it is important for us to remember that *the speaker who is aware of values, value systems, and value postulates in the audience can make wise and important decisions about ways to approach and speak to people.*

Drawing from research in the social sciences, Nugent describes a value "as a conception, explicit or implicit, distinctive of any individual, or characteristic of a group," of what seems desirable. A value influences the making of decisions involving feeling, thinking, and acting. Rokeach adds that a *value is an enduring belief that a specific mode of conduct or end-state of existence is personally or socially preferable to an opposite or converse mode of conduct or end-state of existence.*[5] Values thus seem to indicate how one "would like" and/or "ought" to think, feel, and act.

Research confirms that there are individual and group values as well as general value systems within populations of people. We can therefore identify an American value system, which is still being investigated.

Nugent's components for an American value system are identical with those reported in 1962 by Edward D. Steele and W. Charles Redding. This list continues to be relevant.[6] It serves as a useful example for increasing our understanding of speaking with an audience.

1. *Puritan and pioneer morality.* Many virtues held by the Purtans and the pioneers are held by Americans today. Such virtues include respectability, thrift, self-discipline, cooperation.
2. *Value of the individual.* Many Americans regard the individual as sacred, and see individual needs, attention, and life-styles as being very important.
3. *Effort and optimism.* Work is regarded as a virtue. Hard work is seen as most often rewarded, and as leading to acquisition and ownership of goods and services.
4. *Science and secular rationality.* Americans believe they live in an ordered universe where the environment can be controlled by using reason along with technology and science.
5. *Efficiency, practicality, and pragmatism.* "Getting things done" as efficiently as possible and in practical ways, concentrating on "the here and now," is very important to Americans.
6. *Achievement and success.* It is believed that individual opportunity can provide the industrious and hard worker with status, wealth, power, and happiness.
7. *Quantification.* Largeness, hugeness, vast quantity are terms Americans identify with; events, products, and people are almost larger than life (for example, Superbowl, superstar, superburger).
8. *Material comfort.* Pursuit and achievement of a high standard of living, which brings certain luxuries and comforts to make life both easy and pleasant, is very important.
9. *Generosity and "considerateness."* Americans believe in

basic humanitarianism. This is shown in their support of charities, help for others during disasters, aid for under-developed nations, and in sharing the fruits of their labors.

10. *Rejection and authority.* Virtue is seen in being able to make one's own decisions, in rejection of curtailment of freedom; and in maintaining freedom of choice in such things as occupation, residence, religion, and political activity.

11. *Equality.* Though some inequality has existed and still continues, Americans value equality of opportunity and equal privilege for all.

12. *Change-progress-future.* Nothing is static for many Americans; one ought to continue to move forward, try out the new, "build better mousetraps," and pursue various life-styles.

13. *External conformity.* The approval of others in group living, in working, and in recreation is prized, so that adjustments are often made to gain and maintain approval.

14. *Sociality.* Americans have recognized that they "have to get along" to survive, that friendliness is healthy and rewarding, and that personal and physical mobility is easier through sociability among people.

15. *Humor.* In America humor is often a leveler, so that people can poke fun at themselves, at each other, and at important public figures and institutions. This is considered to be healthy and provides relief from tension.

16. *Patriotism.* The patriot is loyal to the nation and is a good citizen, one willing to defend the nation's traditions and its survival, while contributing to its future. As with other values, patriotism may be approached in several different ways.

These sixteen items add up to a value system. Whether it is individual, group, or societal, a value system is open. It is not easily changed, but new values can be added and old ones can be changed or deleted.

The Reverend Jesse Jackson has in recent years become an eloquent spokesperson for part of the Black Movement in America.

He provides an excellent example of a speaker who appeals to the values of his intended audience. The goal of his recent messages seems to aim at cultivating a generation of young black men and women who are dedicated to black excellence and moral authority.

Jackson's message to black high-school students is the same, according to Michael Putney: "It's time to stop getting drunk, getting high, and getting pregnant. Boys should stop studying Superfly and start studying Shakespeare. Girls should concentrate on their books instead of their bosoms. And together they must realize that sex and violence is not the best definition of what a man and woman ought to be about. The death of ethics is the sabotage of excellence." Jackson is telling his audience to identify certain values and work with them; then the quality and meaning of life for each individual and for black Americans as a group can be tremendously enriched. In fact, Jackson argues: "a revolution in values is in order. A push for excellence."[7]

Combined with Jackson's rhetorical skills and personal charisma, this appeal to values seems to be successful. Putney states: "Whatever or whoever, he touches audiences as few can." He speaks with his audiences from a high moral stance, as a strong advocate for human rights and civil rights. He is effective as a speaker. He centers his speeches on the basic values of his audiences, and explains his idea in light of the values. The importance of values is shown in the behavior of audiences where successful public speakers like Jesse Jackson hold sway.

It is important to keep the connection between values and audience behavior in mind. Understanding the nature of attitude, belief, and value, and learning about their importance to an audience can provide a speaker with important psychological data which can be used to adjust ideas for maximum effect on an audience.

Major Audience-Centered Questions

A speaker ought to raise four basic questions in order to obtain specific information about an audience.[8] To answer the questions requires a substantial commitment from the speaker plus the use of formal and informal methods of inquiry.

1. What does the audience know and how do they feel about the occasion?

An audience, collectively and as individuals, has specific attitudes, beliefs, and values which form the basis of their feelings about the speech they are about to hear, as we have already discussed. Audience responses to the speaker's message are at least partly the result of those opinions they bring to the occasion, the appropriateness of the speaker, and the immediacy of the message. An effective speaker will try to discover the patterns of opinion in the audience. For example, if an audience would like to be anywhere but at a speech, and if the speaker is unaware of this feeling, the hostility that may deaden chances for success can be missed. For example, in a college I attended, students generally felt negative about going to chapel because it was required that they do so. Yet many speakers acted as if the audience was a packed house of eager church-goers. The military services often require their personnel to attend lectures for educational purposes, and speakers need to know how this affects audience response because the attitude of the audience toward the occasion directly affects its willingness to listen.

2. What does the audience know and feel about "me" or who I represent?

This question involves the concepts of ethos and credibility of which we spoke earlier. If an audience does not feel positive about the speaker or knows little or nothing about that person, the specific purpose of the speech will be affected. Positive feelings in an audience are to the speaker's advantage. As a young man in the army Bill found that women in a city near his post were, for the most part, distant, cool, and reticent toward him. He soon discovered the cause; their feelings centered on a negative stereotype of men in the service. He then wore his uniform on the train in order to keep his serviceman's travel discount, but carried civilian clothes with him.

In the city he changed to civilian clothes. Once he had established himself with the townspeople, he would identify himself as a member of the army.

If Billy Graham, John Lennon, or Gloria Steinem came into your speech communication class today, the effect they would have as speakers would be determined largely by your feelings about these people. Similarly, those in a speakers bureau who speak as representatives of a power company which has had severe increases in consumer rates are concerned about how audiences might view them. They must identify how the audience feels about the company they represent. Then they can realistically adjust to these sentiments as speakers.

3. What does the audience know, and how does the audience feel about the subject and purpose for speaking?

A speaker representing the Society for the Preservation of Every American's Rights (SPEAR) intends to get a liberal, racially mixed suburban audience to believe that the federal government is influenced by Communists. The speaker must begin by knowing the audience's views on the subject. A speaker can easily "turn off" an audience by telling them what they already know. Students complain about going through courses and hearing the same information over and over. The professors in question are not tuned into what students know and feel.

A student in a speech communication class spoke to his class about the history of Ping-Pong. This speech could have been interesting, but many in his audience tuned him out when he spoke the obvious—"This is a little white ball, and this is a paddle. The object of Ping-Pong is to hit the ball back and forth across a table and over a net . . ." (Yawn).

4. How does the audience regard itself collectively in a communicative setting?

Audiences are made up of individuals. They are also a collectivity of persons who have particular things in common.

After completing two in-depth studies of the campaigns of political speakers, this researcher became keenly aware of how members of special interest groups behave collectively according to shared feelings about their organizational ritual, their service goals, their political affiliation, and their economic/occupational positions in the community. An audience of Masons, Kiwanians, or members of the League of Women Voters is made up of individuals who have a particular image and group identification. Such an image plays a part in the response of an audience to a speaker and the message.

Each of these questions suggests that the speaker obtain information about what the audience knows and how it feels about the speaker, the occasion, the purpose, and itself. Knowledge and feeling are interrelated in the attitudes, beliefs, and values of people and are also distinctive aspects of individual human personalities. The knowledge a speaker gains from answering these questions can be instrumental in predicting the best way of approaching an audience.

We can think about our own responses to particular speakers on particular occasions. This can provide some useful insight into what we face as speakers.

Realistic images of an audience can also be discovered by studying the dominant "life-style" factors of an audience.

Dominant Life-Style Factors

Research indicates that dominant life-style factors influence audience response to a speaker and the message. Knowledge of the six primary life-style factors gives the speaker a good chance of knowing many of the values and attitudes which shape and form the opinions, positions, and views held within the audience.[9]

These primary factors are:

1. living context
2. age and sex
3. educational level
4. occupational backgrounds
5. religion
6. ethnic roots

Living Context. Looking at auditors' hometowns, individual family situations, and the cultural context in which they live can give valuable clues to a people's attitudes and values. Social scientists have pointed out the effects of urban, suburban, and rural environments on a person's development. People who live their entire lives in the cosmopolitan city of San Francisco would be knowledgeable in different areas and feel quite different from people who spend their lives in the village of Fickle, Indiana. Living context provides a person with self-orientation used as points of reference, comparison, or evaluation when listening to a speech.

Consider the case of Judy, an instructor in urban economics, who taught for the most part at a large university located in the heart of a great city. One night each week she traveled 45 miles to a small regional branch of the university where most of her students came from farms and homes in a rural-agricultural setting. Though Judy maintained the same course objectives for "Introduction to Urban Economics," her approach to the two classes differed considerably.

Many adjustments in her lectures were made as a result of information she gathered about the different living contexts of her student audiences.

Educational Level. Knowing the general level of audience education can be a valuable clue for how sophisticated a speaker's approach to an audience can be. A research firm created a local speakers bureau composed of scientists who would give 25-minute speeches to community audiences. The speakers would also travel around the state in response to invitations. The biggest problem experienced by speakers was adjusting to the educational levels of their audiences. One Ph.D., who worked with physicians doing research on human organ transplants, found that his early speeches were not understood by most of his audience. Taking a "speech training course" offered by his firm, he quickly discovered he had been aiming at an educational level higher than that of his audiences.

Occupational Backgrounds. What jobs members of an audience *do* strongly influences their listening behavior. A Purdue University environmentalist in the department of biology found her speech on the imminent and long-range dangers of pollution a challenge. Her audience came mostly from Hammond, Indiana, a region dominated by the four major steel mills and several oil refineries in the area. They were interested in dealing realistically with problems of pollution, but they also were psychologically tied to economic dependence on big industry. The speaker sought to adjust realistically to the audence's needs and knowledge, especially as her specific purpose related to their occupational backgrounds.

Ethnic Roots. To understand the part ethnic roots plays in public speech communication, one only has to review its dynamic role in the civil rights movement and the white backlash of the 1960s and 1970s. Alabama's George Wallace openly attacked racial integration and federal legislation to force an end to segregation. He frequently appealed to white ethnic sentiment. On a number of occasions in 1964 he traveled in Maryland during the campaign for the Democratic Primary there, introducing a Greco-American, an Italo-American, a German-American, a Slovak-American, and a Polish-American to his audiences to show he had support among ethnic leaders in Alabama. There was a noticeable absence of Afro-Americans on the platform.

Age and Sex. When an elderly political speaker said: "And now I want to speak to the young people in the audience," a middle-aged businessman looked around the auditorium and discovered there were no young people visible. The audience was filled with middle-aged and elderly white couples, smartly dressed for the occasion. The speaker seemed to have drawn an "older crowd." A person's age is often an important factor in audience response. Important attitudes and values tend to become cemented behavior patterns as people reach the later years, and a speaker would have a difficult time changing these attitudes. People relate to life in terms of their age groups and the particular stages they are in.

The sex of an audience also makes a difference to communication. Not too many years ago, when sex roles seemed defined largely by tradition, a speaker would have to adjust his or her remarks according to the sexual composition of an audience. This may still be true for speakers today in terms of how men and women regard themselves. After playing a taped speech to a large student audience, the instructor was challenged by a number of women who claimed the speech was sexist. The instructor had played the same speech as an instructional aid for 4 years. He had disregarded the idea that a speaker ought to discover the sex composition of an audience and determine what implications this has for the speech.

Religion. Although a recent national poll indicated that only 40 percent of the people in the United States attend church, so research has indicated the importance of religious background in audience analysis. Persons feel differently about their religious backgrounds at different stages of their lives and according to their religious needs. Research indicates that religion in American is changing, as are views of religion and human behavior. A speaker must realize that if religion is important to an audience, then it must be examined. Moral codes, religious in nature, often form the core of people's value systems. Arguing for a radical liberalization of abortion laws before a Catholic citizens committee poses unique and difficult problems.

Finally, it is important to categorize kinds or types of audiences. According to Wallace Fotheringham, a most practical way is to view audiences as unintended, intended, irrelevant, and as media channels.[10] The speaker's primary target is the intended audience.

The speaker must also know the basic categories which describe audiences—pedestrian, attracted, selected, discussion group, the absent and captive.

Important Kinds of Audiences

The *intended audience* are those persons for whom a message is particularly designed. In the typical public speaking class, this is often, but not always, the only audience the speaker faces. The purpose is aimed at everyone in class, and speech ideas do not have life beyond the classroom.

Four important kinds of audiences are the intended, the unintended, the irrelevant, and the media channels, as we have seen. While a speaker targets his or her specific purpose for the intended audience, the unintended audience makes up any real or potential opposition to a speaker. The *irrelevant audience* are the aides, colleagues and the like, and mediators for change. These are certainly important persons in any rhetorical situation; however, the speeches are clearly not designed for them. The *media channels* are those who disseminate and diffuse information (either a whole speech, several speeches, or parts of a speech) in an attempt to impart ideas objectively.

Let's consider the case of Charles, a crusading political science major at a municipal university. The university had a policy which prevented announced political candidates from speaking on campus. Charles was among a growing number of students who were angry about this policy and wanted it changed immediately. He and a group of articulate friends formed an ad hoc organization named "Action and Change Today," or ACT. The group received the endorsement of the student government and of many political figures both local and national. The group put together a speakers bureau and a media committee. This committee sent out press releases and bulletins and was charged with the responsibility of encouraging coverage of speaking engagements by the media. Each speaker's purpose was to get the *intended audience* to write, phone, and petition the university administration to change the current policy in exchange for one which would permit *any* political candidate to speak on campus when invited by an organization in the university community.

The intended audience included all students, and supportive faculty and members of the board of trustees. The members of ACT also aimed their message at alumni and parents of students plus local townspeople. Politicians who believed in having a forum for speaking on the campus, but who were not committed supporters, were also part of the intended audience. The intended audience was this broad and diverse, but members of ACT carefully sought, through audience analysis, to identify them.

The unintended consisted of a considerable number of campus administrators, including the president, who were "on record" as having taken a stand to preserve the status quo, plus some faculty members who supported the current policy. One of the local newspapers and radio stations had voiced opposition to change through editorials. These persons of the unintended audience voiced frequent refutations of ACTs messages.

The irrelevant audience consisted of ACT members, another newspaper editorial staff committed to working for a change, and supporters of ACT.

The media channels included persons working for three local newspapers, three radio stations, one television station, the campus press, and radio-television reporters. The members of ACT were aware of two kinds of audience effects: consummatory and instrumental. *Consummatory effects* are both immediate personal satisfaction and other initial responses from auditors to a speaker and a speech. *Instrumental effects* are audience responses which lead to further instrumental behavior. The speaker's objective and specific purpose are clearly aimed at action. ACT sought specific action as its instrumental effect. With the unintended audience there may be undesirable instrumental effects. For example, at Robert's first public appearance, surrogate speakers for the university president accused Robert of a number of inaccuracies in his speech. Robert and his peers countered with other messages designed to achieve desirable instrumental effects with the intended audience. The irrelevant audience offered ACT continued support; they were part of ACT's rhetorical effort. The media channels reported information about the speeches, and published some editorials opposing a change in policy. Persuasion through appeals to the attitudes, beliefs, and values of the audience through the presentation of information was central to ACT's efforts and to those of the opposition. When this particular campaign was complete, ACT had won. Students, faculty, and the board of trustees. voted in favor of change, and a new policy was adopted.

Categorizing audiences is important to the public speaker because it helps the speaker to deal with particular audiences intelligently. A particularly valuable approach was offered by H. R. Hollingsworth in his "Psychology of the Audience." He described six types of audience that exist in relation to speakers. Our study uses five of these categories in a way slightly different from Hollingsworth's[11]: the pedestrian, the attracted, the selected, the discussion group, and the absent. Within these categories there are also members of the intended, unintended irrelevant, and media channel audiences. To prepare ourselves and our speeches well, we must be able to identify and describe audiences with clarity and accuracy.

The *pedestrian audience* is made up of people intent on attending to personal business, but who choose to become part of an audience on the way to somewhere else. For example, at Ohio State, there is a large campus area, the Oval, where "soap box orators" speak in warm weather. On the way from a lecture, I suddenly became part of an audience in the Oval listening to a team of Puerto Rican nationalists advocating independence for their home island. The speakers often found themselves struggling with this audience because persons with a wide variety of opinions, many in opposition to the speakers, were attracted to the event. A pedestrian audience is a real challenge. It requires preparation, strong personal projection, and continued adjustment to the audience.

The attracted audience is a gathering of persons who listen to a speaker because they are attracted to the speaker and/or the subject. One cold and snowing Tuesday a student invited me to hear commentator Paul Harvey. The 2500 people in the Masonic Auditorium, which was packed to capacity, were saying enthusiastic and complimentary things about the speaker. When he walked on stage, a standing ovation reaffirmed the audience's atttraction to him. Most of us are not going to have a following like Harvey's, but we may be speaking on a very attractive topic or occasion which draws a capacity audience. For example, a graduate student very much *unaccustomed* to public speaking was asked to discuss ideas from her dissertation about interpersonal communication in marriage encounter. The speech took place before members of a preschool mother's organization which had not been drawing many women to its quarterly programs. Almost every member attended because the subject of marriage encounter was extremely attractive.

A young attorney, asked to speak at the second annual honors banquet of his alma mater, was astounded when he was faced with a newly built double dining area packed with over 1000 persons. His subject, "Tuition Loans and the Law," had attracted a much larger audience than he had expected.

The *selected audience* is assembled for a common purpose, but not all of its members are sympathetic with each other's or the speaker's point of view. Here we will view a selected audience as one most likely to be sympathetic with the speaker's aim. For example, a former campaign manager for Governor George Wallace of Alabama accepted only speaking engagements in front of "friendly" and "sympathetic audiences" for the 1964 presidential primaries. This was his way of protecting his employer and ensuring enthusiastic audiences for the speaker and news reporters. Audiences were highly partisan and carefully selected.

Women and men in business and industry speak before audiences of selected managers or other company representatives. Knowledge of selectivity can significantly aid the speaker's preparation and presentation of a speech.

The *discussion group*, Hollingsworth contends, enables us to "find the first signs of preliminary orientation toward a speaker." In the discussion group several participants may become the speaker, so the audience is dynamic and transient in its relation to the speaker. For example, a young woman from a large transportation corporation spoke with a small group of community leaders about the loss of the company's credibility in the community. After her 20-minute speech each member of the audience discussed the presentation, and reacted to each other's responses. The speaker was prepared for this kind of interaction. In fact, the company's public affairs office had given her a lengthy list of questions which might be asked and official answers in advance.

Different from all the others, but often of tremendous importance to the speaker, is the absent audience, those who are not actually present, although they are part of the intended audience. They can also be the unintended audience, adversaries the speaker chooses to direct remarks to, knowing that the remarks will be retold by those present at the time.

A law-enforcement public affairs spokesperson offered a "crime prevention seminar" to an upper-middle-class community. The seminar was arranged for a Wednesday evening in the high-school auditorium, and was specifically aimed at discussing burglaries. Only one-third of the room was filled, and because the community had become a high burglary area, the speaker was disappointed in this low attendance. She reshaped her speech on the spot to encourage news reporters to print her belief that crime prevention required the majority of citizens to know about and follow the ideas carefully developed by the police department in relation to crimes of burglary. A second seminar was scheduled 2 weeks later. The audience got the message, and the second seminar was jammed with citizens who had been absent the first time.

In another case a national political figure atacked his absent opponent, knowing that the opponent, his staff, and his followers would see and hear part of this attack in news reports. The speaker had asked: 'Where do you stand on the issues? We've got a right to know! America has a right to know! To some you appear conservative, to others you sound off as a liberal, and to others you create the image of a moderate! You appear to be no one who really offers real and clear solutions to the nation's problems!"

Some moments should also be given to the captive audience, for no other reason, perhaps, than that students in a public-speaking course often consider themselves captive listeners. If attendance in the course is required, perhaps this is so. But captive audiences can also be enthusiastic audience if the speaker makes a real effort to interest and appeal to the wants and needs of listeners. Captive audiences exist both on and off campus. A thorough analysis and subsequent adaptation to such audiences can lead to the same kind of effectiveness possible with the other types of audiences we have examined.

SUMMARY

There are a number of needs expressed by inexperienced speakers: the need to understand the way people in an audience may process information; the need to know about the nature of attitudes, beliefs, and values within audience; the need to know what essential questions must be answered for practical audience analysis; and the need to know about the basic types of audiences. Reponding to these needs can provide the speaker with means of conducting an audience analysis in order to adapt to that audience effectively.

The rational-person approach to viewing an audience was then contrasted with the psychological-person approach. The rational-person approach does not realistically take into account the psychology of the audience, so that the latter approach is advocated. One must do more than view information for a speech in terms of oneself. The needs, knowledge, and factors in the background of the audience must be taken into account when a particular message is designed.

Learning about the psychology of the audience requires knowing about the nature of attitudes, beliefs, and values. Attitude is basically a mental and neural state of readiness, organized through experience and exerting a directive or dynamic influence upon the individual's response to all objects and situations with which it is related. A belief is a psychologically held proposition expressing a degree of faith or acceptance, or the lack thereof. Beliefs are interrelated with attitudes and values. A value is a deep-seated psychological standard which guides a person in approach or avoidance behavior. A value exists with others clustered in a value system which is possessed by each person. Sixteen basic values in the United States serve as useful examples to illustrate standards which guide the thoughts and actions of audience members. Attitudes, beliefs, and values have cognitive, affective, and behavioral dimensions.

An understanding of the concepts or constructs of attitudes, beliefs, and values provides the public speaker with useful information for discovering what patterns of thoughts, feelings, and ideas may exist within a particular audience. Once speakers know the dimensions of attitudes, beliefs, and values, they must discover the dominant ones within an audience, for these are important to the success and effectiveness of a speech. Such knowledge is gained conducting research into the audience to be faced.

Knowing about the psychology of an audience also includes knowledge of information-processing. A practical way of viewing information-processing is to understand how people assimilate and contrast, add and delete, and rationalize in their listening behavior.

These are the basic ways in which we all handle information as it filters into our perceptual thoughts. Unfortunately, processing information can also lead to bending and distorting a speaker's message. Effective communicators do everything they can to find out how information-processing can affect a speech. Such speakers empathize with an audience, speak with clarity, and try to avoid distortion and misunderstanding.

Four major questions are helpful in taking audience-centered, rather than self-centered, steps in speechcraft:

1. What does the audience know and how do they feel about the occasion?
2. What does the audience know and how do they feel about "me" and/or who or what I represent?
3. What does the audience know and how does the audience feel about the subject and purpose for speaking?
4. How does the audience regard itself collectively in a communicative setting?

Life-style factors—which include the living context, age and sex, educational level, occupational backgrounds, religion, and ethnic roots of an audience—help determine audience response to a speaker and the message.

Audiences can be described in a variety of ways; as intended (those people for whom a message is designed), as unintended (those who are in opposition to the message), as irrelevant (those for whom the message is not designed), and as media channels (those who disseminate the message). Audiences can also be classed as pedestrian (those who drop by), attracted (those who respect and like the speaker or the topic), selected (those with a common purpose), discussion group (those who take turns being the speaker), and absent (those not actually present). Captive audiences (those who must attend a speech) are a final category. All these methods of classifying audiences help the speaker to understand an audience and to present a speech as effectively as possible.

We come now to the speech itself. Chapter 4 deals with stating the proposition in a speech and finding supporting information for it. Chapter 5 discusses reasoning with this information to support the speech proposition, organizing the ideas, and using language for maximum effect.

NOTES

1. John J. Makay and William R. Brown, *The Rhetorical Dialogue: Contemporary Concepts and Cases* (Dubuque: William C. Brown, 1972). This approach to processing information is found in chap. 3, "Audience Images," written by Brown.
2. Ronald L. Applebaum and Karl W. E. Anatol, *Strategies for Persuasive Communication* (Columbus: Charles E. Merrill, 1974), pp. 19–59, deal with attitudes.
3. Milton Rokeach, *The Nature of Human Values* (New York: Free Press, 1973).
4. Beatrice Nugent, "The Public Communication of Woodrow Hayes: A Case Study" (Ph.D. diss., Ohio State University, 1974). Chap. 3 is on the dominant American value postulates.
5. Milton Rokeach, *Beliefs, Attitudes, and Values* (San Francisco: Jossey-Bass, 1968).
6. Anyone wishing to read the material should examine Edward Steel and W. Charles Redding, "The American Value System: Premises for Persuasion," *Western Speech,* Spring 1962, pp. 83–91.
7. Michael Putney, "Black Is Dutiful," *National Observer,* May 8, 1976, pp. 1 and 16.
8. These basic questions are drawn from the rhetorical tradition and contemporary applied research. I have used them with success with thousands of students and in industry.
9. The interested student may wish to read Bernard Berelson and Gary Steiner, *Human Behavior: An Inventory of Scientific Findings* (New York: Hartcourt, Brace, & World, 1964).
10. Wallace C. Fotheringham, *Prespectives on Persuasion* (Boston: Allyn & Bacon, 1966), pp. 11–19.
11. H. R. Hollingsworth, "Psychology of the Audience," in *On Speech Communication,* ed. Charles J. Stewart (New York: Holt, Rinehart & Winston, 1971). pp. 148–57.

THE SPEECH: STATING A PROPOSITION AND OBTAINING INFORMATION FOR SUPPORT

In the first three chapters we have determined the general objectives and specific purposes for a speech. We stressed the fact that a speaker, to gain maximum effectiveness and satisfaction, should concentrate on the audience and become audience-oriented. For this we need to know—

1. how to state a proposition which serves our general objectives and specific purpose;
2. how to gather information for supporting material;
3. how to conduct research to obtain this supporting material;
4. how to reason with this information and organize it in the most logical way;
5. how to select the right or most appropriate words to create both interest and meaning.

Chapter 4 responds to the first three needs; Chapters 5 and 6 respond to the other two needs.

A Proposition Is the Core Idea

A proposition can be defined as a sentence which expresses a core idea or a judgment. It makes a claim about whether something is or ought to be. Developing a sound proposition or core statement is the key to developing a sound and purposeful speech.

There are three kinds of propositions: one of policy, one of fact, and one of value. If a proposition maintains that something ought to be, it is a proposition of policy. If a proposition claims something is, it can be either one of fact or value. A *proposition of policy* is a statement that identifies a course of action (a policy) and calls for its adoption. A *proposition of fact* is a statement which asserts that specified circumstances exist. A *proposition of value* is a statement about the goodness, rightness, quality, or merit of something.[1]

A statement that the federal government ought to provide a college or university education for all qualified high-school graduates sets down a proposition of policy as the main idea for a speech. If the main idea were expressed instead as a statement that the earth is being observed by life in unidentified flying vehicles, a proposition of fact would be advanced. A statement declaring that an enlistment in the armed forces is a valuable experience for all eligible men or women is a proposition of value. The points which develop and support a proposition are contentions; they require appropriate data or evidence as additional and necessary support for the proposition. Contentions and support, as evidence, are treated in detail later in this chapter.

The main idea, or proposition, is centered in and aimed at the achievement of a general goal and specific purpose chosen by a speaker. The speaker whose goal is *adoption* would develop a proposition of *policy*. If a speaker persuades an audience in a small community to adopt new and liberal laws about the use of marijuana in the community, the specific purpose would be *change;* the core statement of the message would then be a proposition of policy. If, on the other hand, a speaker wants the audience to *continue* with present laws, either a proposition of fact or value would be developed.

If the principal of an elementary school discovered that a new math program appeared to be largely ineffective, she might argue a proposition of fact before the school board which stated that the current program was not working as planned; or a proposition of value which asserted that the program is not worthwhile. Ultimately, the audience would be faced with a proposition of policy—a change ought to take place.

The goal of deterrence can be argued from two of the three propositions, depending upon the speaker's aim. The friend of a student died as a result of an overdose of an animal tranquilizer which put the friend in a "high" state for several days and utimately led to death. The student gave two speeches in class because of this tragic occurrence. The first sought the goal of deterrence—PSP is a dangerous drug to be avoided by everyone who is a drug-user or potential drug-user. Many in the class knew of the drug, but knew very little about it. Her second speech aimed at *exposition*: educating the class about the very dangerous effects of this drug on human users.

"Being adequately informed on the use of high-protein food supplements is necessary" is another proposition of fact in which the general objective is exposition. *Pleasure* can be supported by any of the three propositions. The key to achieving pleasure is in the nature and function of the speech. The speaker seeks to please the audience by any one of several methods, treating serious topics in light, humorous ways which are acceptable to the audience. Whatever the speaker's goal, maximum meaning and clarity are the results of a well-planned and presented speech. Designing and supporting a proposition are instrumental in the attainment of the desired effect.

Let's now turn to the support to be used by the speaker in identifying assertions, seeing the importance of documentation in a speech, and examining primary kinds of support. We will turn also to major areas for finding support: the library, personal experience, and secondary experience.

Unsupported Propositions

A bare assertion is an unsupported statement and should be avoided. The speaker's responsibility is to express views which can be supported by sound facts and values consistent with what is believed to be true, or highly probable.

A student delivered a fiery 6-minute speech one afternoon in class charging that migrant workers in the city were on the verge of marching to a local plant which canned vegetables the migrants had picked. The migrants planned to burn the plant to the ground, he said. At no time during the speech did he provide any clear evidence for the emotionally charged statements he made. When queried by class members, he confessed the entire speech was based upon a conversation he had had in a bar the evening before. This sort of speaking is shoddy, irresponsible, and in some instances dangerous, because a believing audience may act upon unsupported statements.

Attempting to persuade an audience to *discontinue* its negative attitude toward the actions of the IRA in Northern Ireland, a speaker addressing a group at a Catholic seminary charged that *all* reporting in the American press on the conflict in Northern Ireland was distorted and incomplete. Everyone in the audience knew the purpose of the speech was controversial. A number of students in the audience asked the speaker for evidence or support for his proposition and the points he had made. Nothing but his own general opinion was offered. The audience wanted credible support but received none.

Speakers need to know where in a speech they must clarify and inform the audience and where they must work to provide proof about the ideas being expressed. Evidence as supporting material is crucial for this task.

A realistic analysis of the audience can provide guidance in choosing what must be included or omitted in order to work within the time constraints toward a chosen purpose. Some verbal support can be reinforced by including visual support. Real objects and other visual aids, which strengthen verbal evidence, can be used effectively. Let's first consider verbal forms of support before focusing on the use of visual aids.

Research Supports the Proposition

The student beginning a study of public speaking frequently raises the question: Must I document my speech and cite my sources of evidence? The answer is generally yes. If a speaker is to be perceived as credible, and if the audience is to be made aware of where the support comes from, then the few seconds it takes a speaker to document the data seem necessary. Documentation is important in terms of achieving maximum understanding and acceptance of both speaker and message, especially when the audience knows little about the topic or the speaker.[2]

There are a number of ways and places for research for a speech. Personal knowledge and feelings can be used; interviews can be conducted; information can be drawn from radio and television programs; and the library can be utilized. Because the library is the most accessible and fruitful storehouse of information available, we give it major attention in our consideration of research.

Support for Clarification and Proof

Supporting material is evidence used by a speaker to clarify and/ or prove certain contentions offered to enhance the proposition and achieve the specific purpose for a speech. If a speaker's general goal is adoption, continuance, discontinuance, or deterrence, she or he may present evidence that will clarify information and prove points. If the audience needs little or no clarification, then the speaker may wish to seek only proof and acceptance of the contentions. If the speaker's goals are primarily exposition or pleasure, she or he may choose only to clarify contentions. After completing an audience analysis, the speaker must decide about the nature, degree, and amount of understanding the audience has in light of the rhetorical goal, and must then make a decision about the audience's needs for clarification and proof as far as specific purpose is concerned. A very useful rule for a speaker is: *Clarification precedes proof.* If, for example, a speaker wants an audience to write to its state legislators to request specific changes in consumer-protection laws of the state, the speaker must discover how much the audience knows about the status quo and the positions of the organization in which the speaker is a mediator for change. If the audience is informed, little time need be spent on clarification. Most of the time can then be spent on proof—*creating a high degree of probability that members of this audience will act according to the request.* If the audience generally lacks knowledge relevant to the specific purpose, then clarification as well as proof is needed.

Supporting material consists of a variety of kinds of information considered to be factual and valuable by the speaker and which the speaker believes the audience will also accept as factual and valuable. The most frequently used kinds of supporting material are tangible objects, persons, or events; recorded data; and explanations, analogies, illustrations, statistics, and testimony. Speeches rely mainly on recorded material for support.

Explanation. The explanation is a concise explanatory passage which clarifies an obscure term or concept or describes the relation between a whole and its parts. It calls for clear, descriptive language which generates an image in the mind of the receiver. A speaker might be talking about a concept or view which seems ambiguous, complex, or quite abstract, for example. The best way to clarify is to use an explanation. Consider the speaker who discussed how much she valued love of herself and the people who were part of her life. Early in her speech preparation she realized that the word love has different meanings for different people, and so she sought for a clear explanation which would express her feelings and intentions accurately. A friend suggested she consider the words of Paul, who spoke of love in his Letter to the Corinthians in the New Testament. She decided to use Paul's words to explain what she meant by love:

> Love is patient and kind; love is not zealous or boastful; it is not irritable or resentful; it does not rejoice at wrong, but rejoices in right. Love bears all things, believes all things hopes all things, endures all things.[3]

Paul took the multidimensional concept of love and explained it in a simple and clear way. That is the value of support by explanation.

The speaker found Paul's words to be highly effective with her audience.

Analogy. Analogy, or comparison, points out similarities between something which is known, understood, or believed, and something which is not. A speaker can use two types of analogies: *figurative* and *literal*.

A *figurative analogy* draws a comparison between things which belong to different classes or orders of being. Comparisons of the planet Mars with a spaceship spinning around in the universe or of the human heart with a power plant are examples. A speaker can find the figurative analogy a great help in amplification; but it usually does not establish proof because for validity the phenomena being compared must be *similar* in all ways.

An advocate of zero population growth, Paul Erlich, addressed an audience sympathetic to his views. In order not to confuse his audience, he used forms of support which would both clarify and prove the ideas he advocated. His figurative analogy explains that human growth is increased through declining death rates. It can serve as a meaningful example:

> As a model of the world demographic situation, think of the world as a globe, and think of a faucet being turned on into that globe as being the equivalent of the birth rate, the input into the population. Think of a drain at the base of that globe —water pouring out—as being the equivalent to the output, the death rate of the population. At the time of the Agricultural Revolution, the faucet was turned on full blast; there was a very high birth rate. The drain was wide open; there was a very high death rate. There was very little water in the globe, very few people in the population—only about five million. When the Agricultural Revolution took place, we began to plug the drain, cut down the death rate, and the globe began to fill up.[4]

A *literal analogy* compares things from similar classes which are alike. For example, a speaker could compare one small college with another or one company with another. One student speaker used a literal analogy when speaking to her classmates about the United Nations: "Just as a police force is needed to keep law and order in the United States, so an international police force is needed to keep peace in the world." A literal analogy serves to clarify, but in some cases it can also prove. *If the things being compared are alike in all important ways, then there may be validity in a literal analogy.*

The Illustration. Illustrations are examples which can either be detailed or can lack detail when used in a speech; may be either factual or hypothetical. The *detailed illustration* is a narrative example of an idea or statement to be supported; it describes an occurrence, condition, or event a speaker believes will clarify or prove a point. The illustration which lacks detail is called a *specific instance,* one used with a collection of others which are similar. The *factual illustration* is clearly supported by facts. The *hypothetical illustration* is designed by the speaker and is representative of what could exist or could have existed or could happen or has happened. It has been admittedly fabricated to support a speaker's point.

The illustration is a popular form of support for political speakers. At Kansas State University, where the spirit of the students was refreshed after a football victory which ended a depressing losing streak, and where the figure of Republican elder statesman Alf Landon was familiar, Richard Nixon told the audience:

> Having won some and lost some, I know, as you know, that winning is a lot more fun. But I also know that defeat or adversity can react on a person in different ways. He can give up; he can complain about a world he never made; or he can search the lessons of defeat and find the inspiration for another try, or a new career, or a richer understanding of the world and life itself .When Alf Landon lost to Franklin Roosevelt in 1936, he was not a man to waste his life in brooding over what might have been. In the thirty-four years since then, the world has been transformed. And enriched by his experience, Alf Landon has continued to grow with the world until now he is one of the elder statesmen of America, a man whose wisdom and common sense, and whose out-

spoken concern for the welfare of this nation have inspired and aided generations that have come thereafter.[5]

Besides the hypothetical and factual illustrations utilized, the former president made effective use of specific instances.

Specific Instance. A specific instance is also an example, but one without the detail and narrative required of an illustration. Often time constraint prevents development of many illustrations, so the speaker relies on specific instances for support. These can also serve dramatically to enhance a speaker's point.

Joseph Johnson managed a large company. He spoke to the first-line supervisors one afternoon about the productivity of the plant's employees. He was angry about waste and the falling rate of productivity. At one point in his speech he told the supervisors:

> Look around you far more carefully than you have been doing. I have had trained investigators make unannounced tours through our plant and I have made several myself in recent weeks. What did we see? We saw workers wandering around a great deal when they should have been concentrating on their job and the machinery assigned to them. We saw a number of operations partially maintained because workers were not present and were off for the day, for one reason or another. We saw many of you sitting in offices drinking coffee and having your "smokes" when you should have been doing what your title indicates—supervising! We found one man actually sound asleep on his job in the shipping department, actually standing up but sound asleep. We found others being careless so that when their products came off the line they had to be scrapped because of quality control—their products simply could not be shipped. These are but a few of the things we saw which appalled us and which are contributory to poor productivity in our plant and our falling rate of output!

Whether specific instances are included in our own speeches or are examined in the speeches of others, we can test them by applying questions which are good tests of evidence:

1. Is the illustration closely related to the idea needing support?
2. Is the point or thrust of the illustration obvious?
3. Is the illustration accurate and fair?
4. Does the illustration have strong amplification and/or validation in support of the idea?
5. Is the illustration one to which listeners can relate and with which they can identify?

If all the questions can be answered positively, the illustration being tested is sound and effective.

Statistics. Statistics are numbers which indicate relationships among phenomena or summarize and interpret bodies of data. They quantitatively express facts which have been gathered, tabulated, and analyzed. Statistics may be used to show the proportions of things. If used correctly, statistics can provide powerful amplification and validation. But statistics can be misleading; and they can be used in ways which bore and tire listeners.

When statistics are vivid and clear for listeners, they can create an image and a concept of what the communicator wants each receiver to *understand* and *believe*. An example of the use of statistics to create an image and a concept can be found in a speech by Supreme Court Chief Justice Warren Burger to the American Bar Association:

> There is another factor. It is elementary, historically and statistically, that systems of courts—the number of judges, prosecutors, and of courtrooms—have been based on the premise that approximately ninety percent of all defendants will plead guilty, leaving only ten percent, more or less, to be tried. That premise may no longer be a reliable yardstick of our needs. The consequences of what might seem on its face a small percentage change in the rate of guilty pleas can be tremendous. A reduction from ninety percent to eighty percent in guilty pleas requires the assignment of twice the judicial manpower and facilities—judges, court reporters, bailiffs, clerks, jurors, and courtrooms. A reduction of seventy percent trebles this demand. This was graphically illustrated

in Washington, D.C. where the guilty plea rate dropped to sixty-five percent. As recently as 1950, three or four judges were able to handle all serious cases. By 1968, twelve judges out of fifteen in active service were assigned to the criminal calendar and could barely keep up. Fortunately, few other Federal districts experienced such a drastic change, but to have this occur in the national Capital, which ought to be a model for the nation and a show place for the world, was little short of disaster.[6]

Members of his audience could have asked themselves: Are the justice's statistics substantive proof for his idea that a reduction in the rate of guilty pleas contributes significantly to the increase of demand on the judiciary? Are these figures clear, concise, and pertinent for seeing the problem realistically?

For a further example of this important form of support, we can turn to the scientist talking about problems of world population. He sought to use statistics to help his audience visualize and believe in the severity of problems which are a result of overpopulation in the world. First he explained that the world was experiencing a 2 percent growth rate and that presently there were about 3.6 billion people in the world population. Perhaps realizing the ambiguity of this figure he told his audience.

What can I tell you about 3.6 billion people on the face of the earth? According to any calculations we have been able to make, that is somewhere between three to seven times more people than this planet can permanently support. You say, how can that be? How can we possibly have seven times more people than the planet can permanently support? The answer is very simple. We are supporting those people today, doing a miserable job for about half of them, by doing something very few businesmen would do in the course of their own businesses: burning our capital. We are destroying and dispersing resources that exist in a rather small and finite supply. For instance, we are consuming the fossil fuels which accumulated in the earth's crust over hundreds of millions of years. We will essentially destroy every bit of fossil fuel on the surface of the earth in a period of 200 to 300 years.

We are already wildly overpopulated, by any standard you wish to adopt. But that is not the worst of it, because we have that 2 percent growth rate. A 2 percent growth rate operating at 3.6 billion people a year means that we are adding seventy million people annually to the globe. That means every three years there is another equivalent of the United States to feed, house, and care for on the surface of the earth. To view it by another statistic, in all the wars that the United States has fought, from the Revolution through Laos and Cambodia, we have had roughly 600,000 men killed in battle. The world population is growing so fast that that number of deaths is made up every three and one-half days.[7]

The speaker not only used statistics for support but through analogy he sought to make them significant to his audience. Both speaker and listener could weigh these statistics by understanding what they actually meant.

Statistics can be treated if we ask a series of pertinent questions which focus on the *validity* and *reliability* of the data. The speaker who is using statistics or the audience which must decide what to believe after hearing statistics used in support of an idea can ask these questions in order to check the data:

1. Who is the source of the statistical data? Some sources are more accurate than others; the Gallup Poll and the Harris Poll, for example, are credible.
2. How were the data gathered? Some ask a few persons their opinions on an issue and then generalize to a large population from this highly limited sample.
3. Are the statistics current? Some talk about the overpopulation problem, for example, and rely on statistics 4 or 5 years old.
4. Are the statistics clear? At times, a speaker will list a jumble of meaningless numbers that have little believability or interest for an audience.

5. Do the statistics mean what the speaker thinks they mean? At first glance numbers can be deceiving; what can we *really* infer from them?

A listener can be innocently misled by statistical support, so a careful selection by the communicator who uses the support and an equally cautious reception by the listener is sound.

Testimony. When speakers cite the views of others verbatim, they are using testimony. We all place great stock in the opinion of experts and first-hand witnesses, and that is why testimony is relied upon to such an extent. Courtroom trials and intercollegiate debates are based primarily on the opinions of observers and experts. The credibility of these individuals often determines the outcome of the case. Communicators in day-to-day interaction do essentially the same thing. If a communicator is trying to clarify or prove an idea to an audience, he or she may draw upon a quotation from an authority, which appears far more credible than the personal opinion of the speaker.

One good example of the use of testimony for this kind of purpose can be found in a speech by Gloria Steinem, made early in her support of the women's movement. At one point in a commencement at Vassar Steinem sought to identify feminism with the black struggle for freedom and equality. She used the testimony of the controversial and highly committed Black Panther Bobby Seale, who believed women were socially equal to men.

> For those who still fear that Women's Liberation involves some loss of manhood, let me quote from the Black Panther code. Certainly, if the fear with which they are being met is any standard, the Panthers are currently the most potent male symbol of all. In *Seize the Time,* Bobby Seale writes, "Where there's a Panther house, we try to live socialism. When there's cooking to be done, both brothers and sisters cook. Both wash the dishes. The sisters don't just serve and wait on the brothers. A lot of black nationalist organizations have the idea of relegating women to the role of serving their men, and they relate this to black manhood. But a real manhood is

based on humanism, and it's not based on any form of oppression."[8]

One major question we could raise would be: Is this an expert and/or trustworthy witness? Perhaps a good answer is the following comment:

> Although it is difficult to assess the ethos of Bobby Seale in terms of his being perceived as trustworthy in the minds of the 1970 graduating class at Vassar College, few would probably deny his being an expert on the problem of racial injustice and oppression or Panther in-group behavior. In other words, on these matters the audience probably viewed him as an expert. Many, perhaps, viewed him as being trustworthy as well. Ms. Steinem used Bobby Seale as expert testimony of an oppressed leader who recognized white male discrimination of women by the myths of manhood and who, himself, recognized women as deserving equal rights and treatment as human beings.[9]

Testimony is sound and effective support if it is selected and used carefully. If a situation calls for the testimony of direct observation an expert may not be needed, unless the subject requires a technical specialist to make an intelligent observation. If clarification and proof require expert knowledge and opinion, the speaker must find the most trustworthy opinion available.

How can we judge this form of support? These questions serve as a useful test:

1. What kind of testimony does the idea need for strong support—lay opinion, expert testimony, technical observation?
2. Has the testimony been taken out of context?
3. How biased is the testimony likely to be?
4. Has enough testimony been presented for strong support?
5. Is the testimony from a recognizable and credible source?

Answers to these questions help a speaker and a listener make sound decisions about supporting information.

This kind of support can be vividly displayed with verbal-visual materials. We can discuss various kinds of visual support; together, words and the object or event will clarify and/or prove the thought we seek to convey.

Visual Support

When a speaker is trying to deal with a complex or technical subject, explaining or clarifying seldom enables an audience to understand and remember important details. Perhaps this is because listeners' impressions come only from words, and they are not adequate to convey the speaker's meaning. This inadequacy may be

Co-curricular campus communication expenses

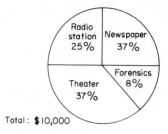

Total: $10,000

repaired by the use of visual support, such as charts, diagrams, graphs, maps, pictures, and models. The verbal is *reinforced* by the visual.

Nevertheless, the attention of the audience should be on the speech and the speaker. Visual aids should assist speakers, not replace them, nor do they serve as opportunities for withdrawal from the audience.[10]

Major Kinds of Visual Support. There are five major kinds of visual support:

1. *Actual Object.* The object being discussed is shown and

Growth percentage of annual sales

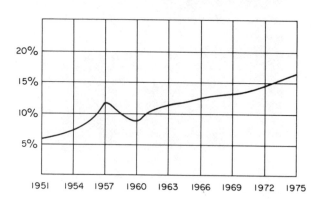

Organization structure Moline State Bank

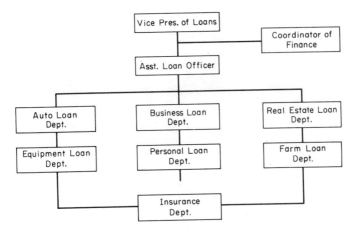

makes ideas more concrete for the audience. Objects are three-dimensional, and this helps to create reality.

2. *Reproductions.* Replicas, mock-ups, and models are three-dimensional, vivid symbols.

3. *Pictorial Reproductions.* Sketches, pictures, photos, and films should be large enough for easy visibility.

4. *Pictorial Symbols.* Diagrams, charts, maps, and important words should be selected with a view to their visibility by everyone in the audience.

5. *Special Apparel.* Costumes, uniforms, equipment, and important paraphernalia for specific and special activities pertinent to the speech can be worn and used.

Visibility, clarity, pertinence, and blending must be guiding concepts for visual supports so that they do not overshadow, distract, or confuse the audience. Some objects, reproductions, pictorial symbols, and apparel are distracting. One student tried to assemble a bazooka in class, and became confused. The object was so cumbersome that he lost the audience. Another student used small charts so complex that almost no one in the audience could see or understand them.

Using Visual Support. Four major principles for choosing visual supports should be kept in mind:

1. *Plan the Use of Visual Aids.* The speaker must decide exactly what materials are needed and precisely where in the speech they will be used. Otherwise the speaker may have a frustrating experience. Visual aids should be planned for the speech and be related directly to it.

2. *Keep the Aids Clear and Simple.* The speaker should not crowd charts with unnecessary details. Include only those details necessary for the clarification of the material to be presented. Eliminate the trivial and unnecessary, and use simple lettering that is easy to read. Use terms which are not ambiguous, and symbols familiar to the audience. Sometimes it is advisable to use several charts with one set of details on each.

3. *Visibility.* Make sure that every bit of information on the visual aid is large enough to be seen by the most distant

viewer. Contrasting colors to differentiate between different classes of detail can be used. All details should be on a large scale, and all lines heavy and broad.

4. *Materials.* Lightweight cardboard or posterboard is good material for preparing diagrams, maps, charts, and so on. Use paint or ink in preference to pencil, so that the lines will be heavy and dark enough to stand out. Many campuses have "sign shops" and art departments eager and willing to help in speech preparation.

Well-planned visual support can be effectively used to fulfill specific purposes. If improperly employed during the speech, these supports can interfere with communication or even make a speaker appear inept. Thus, *considerable thought* should be given to visual support once a speaker determines it can aid in the achievement of a goal.

Keep at least four points in mind:

1. Plan the use of visual aids carefully. (What you will need and where to place them.)
2. Keep the materials clear and simple. (Avoid overcrowding, unnecessary detail, and trivia.)
3. Be certain of visibility. (If everyone cannot see the visual aid it will not be fully effective; make it large, and perhaps colorful.)
4. Use adequate materials. (Avoid aids that are flimsy or cumbersome).

Practice with your visual aids, so that you can use them smoothly throughout your speech. They should be displayed clearly, and handled with ease; you should talk to the audience and not your visual aids. Perhaps the major question to ask is: Will this presentation be just as or more effective without the use of visual aids? If the answer is yes, don't turn to visual materials for assistance. If you determine that your communication can be assisted through the use of visual materials, do not hesitate to employ them.

As a final guide, seven questions are listed below. Study them carefully, and use them often when you prepare to speak. They can also be useful for listening behavior because they can help us examine support by other speakers.

1. Is the support accurate?
2. Is the support directly related to the contention?
3. Is the support relevant to the needs of the audience?
4. Is the support information the audience can understand and accept?
5. Is the support information I can understand and accept?
6. Is the support the best available?
7. Is the contention sound because of the support?

"Attitudes" Are Important Supports

We have now examined the major forms of support. It has been viewed as clarification and/or proof of a line of reasoning offered by a speaker to an audience.

Intercollegiate debaters spend untold hours digging up evidence to support their cases for or against the annual national debate topic. Their use of evidence most often determines whether they win or lose a debate. Members of speakers bureaus in communities across the nation use support to make their propositions clear and informative, or highly persuasive for all kinds of groups. In public-speaking classes, support is used in every presentation to establish the credibility of speakers and their messages.

Support has been described in a variety of ways; for example, it can consist of factual statements originating from a source other than the speaker, such as objects not created by the speaker or opinions of other people offered in support of the speaker's claims. It may consist of evidence intended to induce belief in a proposition. There is also justification for adding an attitudinal dimension to the idea of evidence. Research indicates that *a speaker can link a line of reasoning to the audiences' favorably held attitudes by stimulating such attitudes with the use of vivid and striking evidence.* Evidential attitudes can be considered along with the extrinsic, or outward, and the functional features of support.[11]

We now turn our attention to the process of conducting research for speech communication. Thorough research is crucial if success and satisfaction are to be accomplished in the speaker-audience relationship.

The Library

Besides the college or university library, which seems to provide limitless information for speeches, organizations and companies have libraries which are open to students. Individuals can build their own libraries from which to draw material for speaking and writing. The library is to the speaker what the laboratory is to the scientist, for it is the place where one goes in an effort to discover printed, audio, and visual materials to be used as supporting information for a speech.

An instructor of public speaking had traveled extensively in his city to discover where and what sort of libraries were available to students. The campus provided a central plus several branch libraries. He also found that the two major newspapers in the city had libraries available to the public. Many of the large churches and synagogues maintained libraries of religious materials. Businesses and research foundations had industrial and technological libraries for their employees and would grant special use of much of this information to students. After a thorough canvass of the city the instructor gave his class a useful "hand-out" which mapped the libraries and indicated their probable usefulness to students. Each member of the class was assigned to report on some area in the new campus library—these reports were distributed to everyone in class. The package proved to be a useful guide for student speakers.

As preparations for a speech begin, and the topic and purposes for speaking have been established, numerous libraries can be drawn on for sound, relevant, and up-to-date data to support the ideas that are to be expressed.

First, look at the campus library system. Keep in mind, however, that research for speech materials can lead us inside or out of the community. The campus library may offer books, magazines, journals, newspapers, and other serial publications. In addition, there may be listings for government publications, theses, dissertations, and non-printed materials, such as films, film strips, cassette recordings, and microfilm. The amount of material may seem to be overwhelming; but these general questions and the information help to organize research. If these data are familiar, let them serve as a review as well as a guide.[12]

    1. How are books and other materials listed in the library? Generally, each item has at least three entries filed alphabetically:
       a. authors(s)
       b. title
       c. subject(s)

2. Not all of these entries contain the same information. The author or main entry card has the most complete record of locations, volumes, and other citings.

3. The author or main entry is not necessarily a person. The main entry could be:

   a. an author or editor (Updike, John; Greer, Germaine)

   b. a corporate author (U.S. Dept. of State; International Business Machines Corporation)

   c. a conference or meeting (Conference on Categorical Algebra, University of California, San Diego, 1965)

   d. a standard or uniform title (Grail. Legend; Bible. O.T. Genesis)

   e. the title of the item, when none of these others seems to apply.

4. Usually, a main entry card looks something like this:

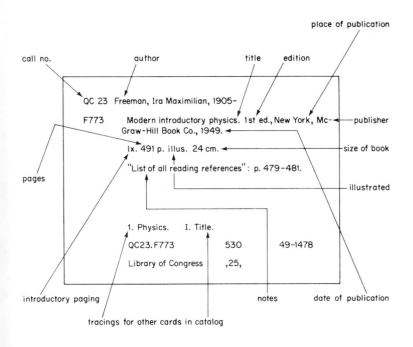

5. Title and subject cards are similar to the main entry card except that the title or subject heading appears on the top line. Subjects are printed in upper-case letters. Remember that complete information concerning locations, volumes, and related matters might not appear on these cards, and you may need to refer back to the main entry card.

6. If you are not sure what the subject listing might be, consult the basic list of subject headings determined by the Library of Congress. Copies are usually available upon request at the reference department or librarian's office.

7. Other helpful hints about subject headings include:
   a. watching for *see* and *see also* references as guides to correct or additional headings that might prove helpful.
   b. being as specific as possible when deciding what to look under (BOTANY not SCIENCE; JUDAISM not RELIGION).
   c. trying a broader heading if you don't find the specific subject you need (DOGS not GERMAN SHEPHEDS).
   d. think of possible synonyms for the subject you first considered.

8. Examples of different kinds of subject headings include:
   a. single terms (GEOLOGY: LIBRARIES)
   b. compound headings (ENGLISH LITERATURE)
   c. phrases (EDUCATION OF WOMEN)
   d. subdivision by type of material (GEOLOGY-DICTIONARIES; LIBRARIES-HANDBOOKS, MANUALS, and so on)
      by place names (GEOLOGY-YOSEMITE VALLEY; LIBRARIES-OHIO)
      by further definition of the subject (GEOLOGY, STRATIGRAPHIC)
      by addition of dates (ENGLISH LITERATURE-19th CENTURY; GEOLOGY, STRATIGRAPHIC-PLEISTOCENE)

   Names, personal or corporate, may be used as subjects, as well as authors (SHAKESPEARE, WILLIAM, 1564–1616 —TRAGEDIES).

9. With so many types of cards cross-filed, there are basic filing rules that can be used to help find what we're looking for:
   a. When the same word is used for a person, place, subject, or in a title, cards are filed in that order.
   b. The order of subjects is indicated in this example:
   EDUCATION
   EDUCATION-MICHIGAN
   EDUCATION-1975
   EDUCATION, HIGHER
   Education of a gentleman. (title)
   EDUCATIONAL PSYCHOLOGY
   c. Articles in English, such as a, an, and the, and their foreign language equivalents, are ignored in filing when they appear at the beginning of a title.
   d. Abbreviations, such as Dr., Mrs., and St., are filed as if they were spelled out (Doctor, Mistress, Saint).
   e. Modified vowels, such as ä, ö, and ü, are filed as if they were spelled ae, oe, and ue; M', Mc, and Mac are filed as if they were all spelled Mac.
   f. Numerals are filed as if they were spelled out (*100 stories* is filed as *One hundred stories; 1984* as *Nineteen eighty-four.*)

10. When you find the card you need, copy down the complete call number, including all the letters, numbers, and dates. These comprise the item's unique identification number. Also note any locations given on the card. If you are not sure how to obtain the item using this information, ask for assistance at the circulation or other desks designated to help library users.

Journals, government documents, and newspapers are excellent sources of information for the speaker. Consider basic information often requested about the use of these materials. Speakers should try to draw on journals and government documents for supporting data.

Journals

1. Journal articles are not generally indexed in the public card catalogue. The card catalogue is the index to book and journals and titles; printed periodical indexes reveal the contents of the journals. The number of journals an index will cover varies from a few to a few thousand!

2. There are two major types of periodical indexes: Those which give only the citation, and those which also give an abstract or summary of the article. Some indexes which give only citations are: *Applied Science and Technology Index, Art Index, Business Index, Education Index,* and the *Reader's Guide to Periodical Literature.* Some indexes which also give abstracts are: *Biological Abstracts, Chemical Abstracts,* and *Psychological Abstracts.*

3. Most periodical indexes are found in the reference sections of campus libraries and may be used in the library. The main library reference room has the largest selection of indexes, but if there are department libraries, each department library has those most useful to the subject areas in which they collect. The indexes will be listed in the card catalogue of the library.

4. Indexes are not difficult to use. Instructions are usually printed inside each issue or inside the cumulated year volume. The author listing and subject sections are alphabetical. Subject indexes may be arranged by a preselected term or by key words from the title. In either case, the user may have to "shop around" before finding the terms which are wanted.

5. It is a good idea to note the entire citation and to use the same format for each citation. Remember to check in the front of the index to find out the full title of the journal; abbreviated titles are very difficult, if not impossible, to locate in libraries. It may also be helpful to note the number of pages in the reference, and whether illustrations or bibliographies are included.

6. Most of the major journals indexed will be available on cam-

pus. To determine if the library has a journal, check the listings and consult with library personnel if you have questions.
7. Journal circulation policies vary. Generally, journals are used
   in the library; at times they can be charged out.
8. Current issues of journals are usually shelved separately from
   the bound volumes. Note the date of the volume needed so
   that locating the volume or issue is made easy. Some locations shelve by the call number, and some shelve alphabetically by title.
9. A journal volume not on the shelf may be in circulation, at
   the bindery, in the process of being reshelved, in use at the
   moment but not charged out, or it may simply be missing.
   Check with the circulation desk.

Government Documents
1. Many libraries receive most major U.S. government documents. The more important ones are catalogued and are
   placed in the stacks or in appropriate department libraries.
   To find them, look in the card catalogue under the issuing
   agency, the title, or the author, if you know one. Study this
   example of the way agencies are listed:

   U.S. Dept. of Labor. Manpower Administration. HD 5723
   Manpower research and development projects. 1971-A2772
   ed. (Washington)
2. If the material needed is not in the library's listings, check in
   the reference department. Many of the less important government documents are not catalogued in the regular way.
3. If a particular author or title is unknown but the researcher
   wants to look at documents published about a certain subject, check the *Monthly Catalog of U.S. Government Publications,* which is usually available in a reference room or at
   other library locations. It is arranged alphabetically by organizational division, listing the output of each agency of the
   government for that month. The index is called the *Cumulative Subject Index to the Monthly Catalog of U.S. Govern-*

ment Publications; it combines subject listings in alphabetical order.

4. Legislative material can be found in the reference department. Ask for federal and state bills, U.S.; Congressional committee hearings and reports or the *Congressional Record*; or other legislative sources.

5. The number of documents from foreign countries in a library varies considerably, depending on the extent of each library's holdings.

Newspapers

1. To find out if a particular newspaper is currently received anywhere on campus, call or stop by the library. Only selected newspapers are received, and storage problems prevent keeping extensive back files.

2. Newspaper articles on particular topics can be located in several indexes. The *Christian Science Monitor Index, New York Times Index*, and the *Newspaper Index* (including the *Chicago Tribune, Los Angeles Times, New Orleans Times-Picayune*, and the *Washington Post*) are some of the indexes often received on campus. Check the name of the newspaper in the card catalogue to see if the library has it on microfilm and/or receives an index for it. When working on a national or international topic, you may use the *New York Times Index* as a general index to gauge approximately when the event occurred; this will give you an idea of when newspapers would have carried the story. Newspaper indexes usually take four to six months to be published, so immediate information is not available through them.

3. *Facts on File* is a weekly summary of world news. It is usually received one or two weeks after the week's events, and it has a subject index.

4. To find out what newspaper editorials have been saying on a particular subject, look into *Editorials on File*. With a format similar to *Facts on File*, it includes selected editorials on vari-

ous subjects from the nation's newspapers. It is published about six weeks after the newspaper publication.

5. *Alternative Press Index* includes "alternative and underground publications" and gives information on underground newspapers. There is a long time lag in the publication of this index.

Audiovisual Materials Available in the Library

Libraries spend vast sums of money annually for equipment that shows films and television programs and plays recordings. It is not uncommon to walk through a modern campus library and see films shelved and catalogued alongside books, where people sit quietly in booths with headsets listening to a cassette or watching a historical account on a screen built into the booth. With these materials quotations can be transcribed and notes taken for inclusion in speeches, and actual audiovisual material can be used during presentations before an audience. A great deal of material is found on microfilm, an extremely fine way of keeping information stored and available.

An excellent listing of references is offered by Gruner, Logue, Freshley, and Huseman in *Speech Communication in Society*. The information on indexes, yearbooks, statistics, dictionaries, encyclopedias, biographical data, newspapers, magazines, atlases, and government publications can be of great value to speakers.[13]

Indexes in which articles on many different topics are listed by either subject or author or both are given below. *Business Periodical Index* will give a speaker the location of articles published on "communication" in business in 1960, for example. The author, date, journal, article title, volume, and page of each article is given.

> *Ulrich's International Periodical Directory.* Approximately 30,000 periodicals are classified by subject. Indicates where the periodicals are indexed.
>
> *An Index to Indexes*, 1942, Norma Olin Ireland. "Indexes, as separate publications, date their development only back to

the nineteenth century . . ." "Our purpose is to assemble into one volume a selection of *published* indexes . . ." Includes special indexes (*Index to Poetry and Recitation*, etc.), indexes to sets of books (*Great Debates in American History*, 1913, etc.), periodical indexes (*Magazine Subject Index*, etc.), cumulative indexes to individual periodicals (*National Geographic Magazine*, etc.), government document indexes (*Index to Farmers' Bulletins*, etc.).

Local Indexes in American Libraries, 1947. Calls attention to "approximately 8,000 indexes" which "were submitted from 950 libraries." Whereas *Index to Indexes*, above, contains published indexes, this work includes *unpublished* indexes.

Readers' Guide to Periodical Literature, 1900 to date. Indexes articles appearing in more than 100 well-known periodicals in general fields. Notes which of the journals are available in braille or on tape.

Biological and Agricultural Index, 1916 to date. Indexes articles dealing with agriculture and related fields.

Art Index, 1929 to date. An index to a selected list of art periodicals and museum publications, covering both the fine and applied arts, including archaeology, architecture, ceramics, graphic arts, painting, sculpture, and landscape architecture.

Business Periodicals Index, 1958 to date. Indexes periodicals in the fields of business and industry.

A Guide to the Study of the U.S. of America. Representative books reflecting the development of American life and thought. Mugridge, Donald H., and Blanche P. McCrum.

Writings on American History, 1902–. List of books and important articles on all phases of American history. A gap remains during World War II years.

Index to the Writings on American History, 1902–1940. Index to work listed immediately above up to 1940.

The Encyclopedia of American Facts and Dates. Carruth, G. et al. 4th ed., 1966.

Education Index, 1929 to date. Covers educational periodicals, books, and pamphlets.

Applied-Science and Technology Index, 1913 to date. (Formerly *Industrial Arts Index*). Indexes journals, books, and pamphlets in the fields of technology and physical sciences.

Social Sciences and Humanities Indexes (Formerly *The International Index to Periodicals*.) 1907 to date. Covers scholarly journals in the humanities and social sciences.

New York Times Index, 1913 to date. A subject guide (and author, if any) covering all articles that have appeared in *The New York Times*.

Public Affairs Information Service, 1915 to date. Commonly known as *PAIS*. Indexes periodicals, books, pamphlets, and documents in the fields of sociology, public affairs, and business.

The Vertical File Index, issued monthly and helpful in locating pamphlet material published by a variety of organizations.

Cumulative Book Index (successor to the *United States Catalog*). Includes a record of nearly every book published in the U.S.

Catalog of the Theatre and Drama Collections, New York Public Library. More than 120,000 plays written in western languages appear in this catalog. By author and subject.

Music Collection, New York Public Library. Thirty-three volumes plus supplementary materials.

A Check List of Cumulative Indexes to Individual Periodicals in the New York Public Library. A cumulative index is to be understood as one which indexes at least three volumes of a file, and makes at least a slight attempt at the classification of the periodical's contents.

British Humanities Index, 1962 to date. Superseded the *Subject Index to Periodicals* which had been published since 1915 (with exception of the years 1923–25). More than 250 periodicals covered by author and subject.

The Metropolitan Museum of Art, New York. This twenty-four volume catalog represents in book form the 147,000 volumes in this library.

Avery Index to Architectural Periodicals (Columbia University). "To comprehend architecture in its widest sense," including archaeology, decorative arts, interior decoration, furniture, landscaping, architecture, planning-and-housing.

Cumulated Magazine Subject Index, 1907–1949. A cumulation of the forty-three volumes of the *Annual Magazine Subject Index* which is now largely out of print. Designed to complement *Readers' Guide, Poole's Index,* and *Annual Library Index.* As early as 1907 covered seventy-nine American and English periodicals, with some emphasis on local and state history.

Engineering Index

Biography Index

Index to Latin America Periodical Literature

Catholic Periodical Index

The Art Institute of Chicago

Index to Legal Periodicals

Industrial Arts Index

London Times Index

Occupational Index

Poole's Index to Periodical Literature, specially useful for articles published before the *Readers' Guide* was begun in 1900.

Book Review Index

Essay and General Literature Index

Granger's Index to Poetry

Ottemiller's Index to Plays in Collections

Bibliographic Indexes. Each cumulative yearly edition includes more than four thousand bibliographies on numerous topics.

Stevenson's *Home Book of Quotations*

John Bartlett's *Familiar Quotations*

Mencken's *A New Dictionary of Quotations on Historical Principles from Ancient and Modern Sources*

Oxford Dictionary of Quotations

Cyclopedia of Practical Quotations, Hoyt

YEARBOOKS AND STATISTICAL INFORMATION

Yearbooks are publications, usually issued annually, that contain concise up-to-date facts and statistical information. Some of the many in your library are:

Ayers' Directory of Newspapers and Periodicals

Statesman's Yearbook: Statistical and Historical Annual of the States of the World, 1864 to date.

Statistical Abstract of the United States, 1878 to date. Published annually by the U.S. Bureau of Foreign and Domestic Commerce, is a "summary of authoritative statistics showing trends in trade and industry, as well as social progress."

World Almanac and Book of Facts, 1868 to date.

Facts on File

Information Please Almanac, 1947 to date.

Monthly Labor Review, data concerning payrolls, employment, cost of living, retail prices, industrial disputes.

Survey of Current Business, data on domestic and foreign trade, exports, imports, etc.

The Commerce Yearbook, provides information about business conditions in the U.S.

Representative American Speeches, 1937 to date, published annually, contains selected speeches made each year.

The Americana Annual, covers current events and biographical items for each year.

Britannica Book of the Year

New International Yearbook

World Book Encyclopaedia Annual

SPECIAL DICTIONARIES AND ENCYCLOPEDIAS

Encyclopedia of the Social Sciences

Oxford Classical Dictionary

Cassell's Encyclopaedia of Literature

Thorpe's Dictionary of Applied Chemistry

Hastings' Encyclopedia of Religion and Ethics

Webster's Geographical Dictionary

Oxford English Dictionary

Good's Dictionary of Education

Dictionary of Speech Pathology (1970, Moore Publishing Co., Durham, N.C.)

Encyclopedia of Educational Research

Jewish Encyclopedia
Catholic Encyclopedia

BIOGRAPHICAL INFORMATION

Who's Who (British)
Who's Who in America
Who Was Who in America
International Who's Who
Current Biography
Webster's Biographical Dictionary, famous persons of all time
  plus pronunciation
Twentieth Century Authors
Directory of American Scholars
American Men of Science
Dictionary of American Biography (noteworthy dead)
Dictionary of National Biography (United Kingdom, dead)
Who's Who in American Education
Leaders in American Education
Who's Who in Engineering
National Cyclopedia of American Biography

NEWSPAPERS

For close-up pictures of the past and present, you will want
to consult local and national newspapers in your library; many
of these will be on microfilm. The book, *Newspapers on
Microfilm*, lists approximately 21,700 entries, representing
4,640 foreign newspapers and nearly 17,100 domestic.

Atlanta Constitution	*The Boston Globe*
Chicago Daily Tribune	*The New Orleans*
The Christian Science Monitor	*Times-Picayune*
London Times	*Washington (D.C.) Star*
Manchester Guardian	*Louisville Courier-Journal*
New York Herald Tribune	*Des Moines Register*
(now out of print)	*Los Angeles Times*

The New York Times	*Minneapolis Star*
Portland Oregonian	*Omaha Bee*
St. Louis Post-Dispatch	*Denver Post*
The Wall Street Journal	*San Francisco Chronicle*

MAGAZINES

The American Scholar	*Monthly Labor Review*
The Atlantic	*Financial World*
Fortune	*Current Events*
Harper's Magazine	*Annals of the American*
The Nation	*Academy of Political and*
Newsweek	*Social Sciences*
The Reporter	*Current History*
Saturday Review	*National Geographic Magazine*
Time	*Yale Review*
United Nations Review	*North American Review*
U. S. News and World Report	*United States News*
Vital Speeches	*American Economic Review*
New Republic	*Barron's Weekly*
	Foreign Affairs

ATLASES

Atlases contain carefully indexed maps and statistical information.

Rand McNally Commercial Atlas
Encyclopaedia Britannica World Atlas
Adams' Atlas of American History
Westminster Historical Atlas to the Bible

GOVERNMENT PUBLICATIONS

The United States government publishes numerous documents on agriculture, education, labor, and many other topics you may be interested in. Your library, particularly if it is a "government depository," will have many of these materials. Publications of the bureaus and departments of the federal government are indexed in *Monthly Catalog of United States Government Publications.* Many of the government's publications can be ordered from Superintendent of Documents, Government Printing Office, Washington, D.C.

Taking Careful Notes

Once a speaker begins reading for information, taking notes becomes very important. There are many techniques for note-taking, and each person can establish his or her own. Five-by-eight-inch ruled or plain cards seem to be most useful in gathering data for speech preparation. These provide adequate writing space, and are easy to handle and sort when the classification and grouping phase comes.

Generally speaking, a speaker should restrict each card to a single idea or topic. A card may contain a single fact, example, or quotation with its appropriate heading.

PERIODICAL

Topic

CONTEMPORARY EDUCATION

Source

Harvey, Thomas R., "A Heritical Approach to Evaluation," **Journal of Higher Education,** November, 1974, pp. 628–634. This information is on p. 630.

Information

BOOK

Topic

FEMINIST MOVEMENT

Source

Carden, Maren, L. **The New Feminist Movement.** Russell Sage Foundation, 1974. This information is on pp. 110–111.

Information

For sound documentation, always indicate the source, the date, and the page before taking detailed notes. The information may be used in the final speech or in checking for additional research. If a question-answer period is included in a communication experience, some members of the audience may request specific references.

Tour the Library Completely

Libraries vary considerably according to the size of a college or university. It is important to become familiar with the particular library system to determine how it can serve students in speech communication. Practice in using the card catalogue, the physical location of particular subjects in the library stacks, and what kinds of information are available in the reference area are important items for public-speaking students. Learning how to use the library effectively, and consultations with the library staff about finding and using information, can save considerable research time. Many students waste time wandering aimlessly about a library because they do not know how to use it effectively. Students unfamiliar with the library system on and off campus may offer audiences weak and unsupported messages simply because they have avoided using any library at all.

In addition to libraries, research for speeches should be conducted by examining personal and secondary experiences. An excellent discussion of these sources is provided by Mudd and Sillars in *Speech: Content and Communication.*[14] They focus on personal experience as a resource for building a speech.

Personal and Secondary Experience as a Resource

No other person can look back to precisely that same set of experiences you have had. Your life, the things you have done, and the things that have happened to you are unique when they are viewed as a whole. This uniqueness in your own personal experience has important implications for your speaking. First, there are some things that you know more about than anyone else. This special knowledge alone qualifies you to speak authoritatively about some subjects. A second consideration, however, qualifies the usefulness of your unique knowledge: Not merely have no two persons had identical experiences; indeed, very few of your experiences have been shared by everyone. Consequently, that which is most valuable in your experience, its uniqueness, is also the most difficult to communicate. Successful communication demands a common ground of shared experience in order to bring about identification between you and an audience. Although you may, for example, know more about automobiles, teenage language habits, or ice hockey than any member of your audience, you can use your own personal experiences in communicating this knowledge to others only if you help your audience to interpret these experiences in the light of their own personal and unique backgrounds.

Good speakers sense readily which of their own experiences are common to other people. When they draw on these common experiences and interpret them intelligently, they achieve clarity and create interest through this common bond. If you recognize both the advantages and the limitations of personal experience as a source of supporting material, you can use this kind of material to bring clarity and interest to what you say. You can go back into your own past and select material that makes it possible for you to explain your ideas with the accuracy and precision of immediate knowledge. If you draw on your own experience, you can select material that helps an audience to perceive your ideas in concrete form. Anyone who has worked on an assembly line has absorbed countless minute details that could never come secondhand. Vivid recollection of these details can supply material that would not be available from the most meticulous research.

The knowledge gained from examining what others have thought and done can be called secondary experience. Such information is necessary because frequently people must speak on subjects with which they do not have direct personal experience. Many have not been Blacks, Jews, Catholics, forest rangers, United States senators, or social workers. Consequently, personal experience must be supplemented by examining the experience of others.

When you do not find in your own background some personal experience to lend vividness to your idea, you can draw from what someone else has written or said an experience that *could* have happened to anyone, including every member of an audience. This kind of supporting material brings clarity to your ideas because it brings them within the comprehension of the listener. It adds interest to the speech because it has the immediacy of direct, personal experience.

Being dependent upon others for information, however, is always a potential danger. Some of the difficulties of audience acceptance that arise in using secondary experience as speech material have been discussed in the preceding chapter. The further point is to be made here that even when you choose speech materials carefully, the definitions, examples, statistics, and testimony you gather from sources outside your experience are always subject to bias. No matter how meticulous you may be in trying to maintain an objective attitude toward a subject (and this you will seldom be able to do), the external sources you consult are as susceptible as you are to personal bias.

It is extremely doubtful that all bias can be removed from any extended discourse. The very fact that you *select* the material you use, elect to use one datum and to dispense with another, automatically builds into a speech an inescapable bias. Even reports appearing in the news magazines and newspapers, theoretically intended to present an objective statement of newsworthy events, often demonstrate the editorial bias of the publication in which they appear. The evil in bias lies not in its being present but in its not being recognized. In order to detect the bias that will almost necessarily be present even in the writing and speaking of those who are concerned with what they say, study many sources of information.

Beyond the need to be on the lookout for the bias of any source of information you consult, using the experiences and ideas of others for speech material requires you to evaluate what you hear and read. You must learn to listen and read with maturity and judgment. To be ill-informed may be even worse than to be uninformed.

When they are thoughtfully evaluated and properly used, secondary materials will form a good basis for helping a listener to identify himself with your ideas. Remembering that secondary experience must have the vividness and the immediacy of direct personal experience, we present some of the ways in which this kind of supporting material can be found.

Conversations and Interviews

The conversations you have with friends will frequently provide material for a speech. Even the ideas with which you disagree can be useful; they may be examples of concepts prevalent in our society.

Frequently you will know of some expert, perhaps a faculty member or someone in the business community, who can help you to understand a more complex subject. You may be surprised to discover how willing people are to help you. Remember, their fields of specialization are important to them and they are usually pleased to know that they are of interest to others. Faculty members, for instance, feel a bit flattered when students ask for help in finding materials.

When you solicit information from others, however, it is wise to be sure you know what you want to ask. Begin thinking seriously about your subject sometime in advance. Do some reading before you approach the person you want to interview. Arrange an appointment. Say what you will need to know, and the limits of the subject you intend to speak about. Give the person you interview time to think about your questions. Then, when you have the interview, be prepared to ask specific questions. These will form the framework of the interview. You can expect to be disappointed with an interview that begins like this: "What can you tell me about electronics? I gotta give a speech tomorrow."

Radio, Television, and Lectures

Radio and television programs can be valuable sources of speech material. You will find, however, that gathering useful data from broadcasts is more difficult than gathering them from an interview. The major problem, of course, is that you can't ask questions. Accordingly, you must be more careful in listening and in taking any notes you may want to keep for future reference.

In many instances, radio and television programs offer data that would otherwise be unavailable. It is not likely that a college student could approach the U.S. president, for instance, and ask him for his views on the relations of this country with the Soviet Union, or federal aid to education, or government support of a program of medical care for aged citizens. Yet the president's views are often communicated to the nation at large over radio and television. Some statements made under these circumstances will not appear in print, since many newspapers do not report the complete text of speeches broadcast on radio or television.

To make the most of an opportunity to gather speech materials from broadcasts requires much the same kind of preplanning that is done for interviews. You may discover that the Egyptian ambassador is appearing on a public affairs broadcast. Because you are preparing a speech in which the background of Arab-Israeli conflict is pertinent, you will plan to listen. If you have some early planning in your speech, you will know the kinds of things to listen for.

Public lectures, not broadcast, are information sources less often available than broadcasts, but their content is often especially valuable. Even college lectures may supply excellent speech material.

Note taking is an important skill to acquire. Anyone who can write can take notes of one sort or another. Taking good notes requires not only the ability to listen well, but it also demands some general background in the subject at hand. Otherwise, it is difficult to make a proper distinction between what is essential and what is not. Indiscriminately made notes are either unnecessarily voluminous because they are filled with unimportant data, or they are too sketchy because the notetaker fails to put down important facts.

A practice that is helpful in taking notes is to keep paper and pencil near at hand. Some people carry a notebook with them at all times so that they can jot down ideas as they occur. In this way, otherwise vagrant and fleeting thoughts, references, examples, and quotations can be captured and preserved.

When primary and secondary experience is used as research for obtaining support, notes can be taken in the same way as in library research. Note cards which include topic, source, and information are filled out.

SUMMARY

Three major needs of a speaker who is preparing a message for an audience were considered. These needs are common to all communicators:

1. to state a proposition which can serve the *general* objective and the *specific* purpose for speaking
2. to know what kind of information is most practical as supporting material for speaking on a proposition
3. to conduct research in order to obtain the necessary supporting material

Essentially, a proposition is a core idea and a judgment expressed in words. There are three types of proposition from which a speaker can make a choice: a proposition of fact, a proposition of policy, or a proposition of value. These easily relate to particular general objectives—adoption, continuance, discontinuance, deterrance, exposition, and pure pleasure. A proposition must be aimed at both the general objective *and* the specific purpose, or precise response, a speaker wants from an audience.

Propositions need maximum support if they are to escape being assertions without clarification and/or proof. Audiences seem to be more receptive to and influenced by messages based on sound support and documentation. Someone faced with the preparation of a speech can profit greatly from knowing what kinds of support seem most suitable and useful for communication. These include explanation, analogy, illustration, specific instance, statistics, and testimony. All supporting material can be tested through the use of the pertinent questions and assertions, included here. Support may also be visual and in the form of an actual object, a reproduction, a pictorial reproduction, a pictorial symbol, or special apparel. Care must be taken in the preparation and use of visual support so that it contributes effectively to the message of the speaker.

Obtaining support for a proposition usually entails conducting research in various ways. Perhaps the best source of information is the library. In a sense, the library is the speaker's laboratory. Use of various libraries for the preparation of a message was described, and a practical procedure for taking notes was given. Speakers are encouraged to collect data on cards (preferably five by eight inches in size), which include the topic, the source, and the selected information.

Other areas for conducting research include personal experience; secondary experience; conversations and interview; and radio, television, and lectures.

NOTES

1. Charles Mudd and Malcolm Sillars, *Speech: Content and Communication,* 3rd ed. (New York: Thomas Y. Crowell, 1975), pp. 22–25.

2. Helen Fleshler, Joseph Ilardo, and Hoan Demoretcky, "The Influence of Field Dependence, Speaker Credibility Set, and Message Documentation on Evaluation of Speaker and Message Credibility," *Southern Speech Communication Journal,* Summer 1974, pp. 389–402.
3. 1 Cor. 13:4–7.
4. Speech by Paul Erlich to the First National Congress on Optimum Population and Environment, June 9, 1970, in Chicago, Illinois.
5. Speech by Richard Nixon, Kansas State University, September 16, 1970.
6. Speech by Warren E. Burger, American Bar Association, August 19, 1970, in St. Louis, Missouri.
7. Speech by Paul Erlich.
8. Speech by Gloria Steinem, "Living the Revolution," Commencement at Vassar College, 1970, Poughkeepsie, New York.
9. John J. Makay and William R. Brown, *The Rhetorical Dialogue: Contemporary Concepts and Cases* (Dubuque: William C. Brown, 1972), p. 332.
10. The information on visual aids is written from standard instructional materials I have distributed to students for "The Communication of Ideas and Attitudes."
11. Victor D. Wall, "Evidential Attitudes and Attitude Change," *Western Speech,* Spring 1972, pp. 115–23.
12. The information on the library has been adapted from that offered by The Ohio State University Library, 1975.
13. From Charles R. Gruner et al., *Speech Communication in Society* (Boston: Allyn & Bacon, 1973), pp. 69–75. Reprinted with permission from the publisher.
14. Mudd and Sillars, *Speech: Content and Communication,* pp. 134–36. Reprinted with permission from the publisher.

CHAPTER 5

THE SPEECH–REASONING AND ORGANIZATION

Carefully examine eight propositions taken from public speeches:

I want all of you to understand why we want you to study botany.

I can't understand why this college has requirements which force me to take botany when my major is philosophy.

U.S. senators are all a bunch of crooks!

U.S. senators, for the most part, are outstanding public servants.

Euthanasia is a way to allow death with dignity.

Euthanasia is a form of murder.

I'm going to explain to you what I think it means to be an employee of Huntington.

No matter what is said, I don't care what it means to be an employee of Huntington beyond what I can earn in salary.

In order for speakers to avoid the danger of unsupported assertions, supporting information is needed to clarify and/or establish proof about each proposition. Chapter 4 discussed support. Now it is time to examine how to use support to give strength to propositions which develop from the general objective and specific purpose chosen by the speaker. We also can explore ways of organizing units of reason for a speech and we can pay special attention to a consideration of our choice of words for an audience.

Reasoning is the process of using known or believed information to explain or prove other statements less well understood or accepted. It is the process which goes from what we know to what we declare or conclude. Some reasoning deals with controversial ideas, and some does not. For example, a speaker could be arguing that it is wrong to think that life begins at the moment of conception. Reasoning would certainly be important in this speech. One could explain the process of photosynthesis and its importance for sustaining life on earth, and this would also require careful reasoning. The reasoner tries to achieve both a general objective and a specific purpose with an audience. If the reasoning is controversial the speaker tries to persuade; if the reasoning is not controversial, the speaker seeks to be completely understandable. In some instances, both controversial and noncontroversial speeches would strive for high degrees of persuasion and complete understanding.

Study Fig. 5-1. The arrows are marked by various degrees of understanding and belief in an audience. The speaker's aim is for the desired response.

The Toulmin Approach

According to Carroll Arnold, from an audience's vantage point a speech is a series of interrelated, assertive forces which are displayed for their interpretation and evaluation.[1] The speaker who seeks to *reason* carefully ought to focus on the pathways in the audiences' minds when they are asked to understand, accept, and do something. A useful audience analysis can provide needed information about the audiences' minds. As speakers, we must find the best way to reason with a particular audience.

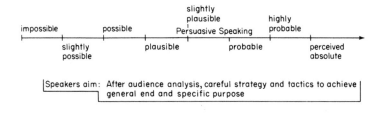

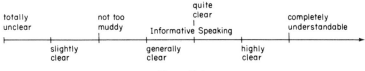

Figure 5-1.

The speaker and the audience can reason together. Ideally reasoning should be sound and accurate. We should reason from *contentions,* which are *supported* statements subordinate to the *main idea* or *proposition* offered to an audience. Let us now concern ourselves with the elements of reasoning which provide principles for communication.

Perhaps one of the best approaches to reasoning was originally developed by Stephen Toulmin in *The Uses of Argument.*[2] Although the Toulmin approach can become complicated, it can be used in a basic and practical way. As an audience-centered guide for reasoning, it should be put into practice frequently when we design our speeches.

A line of reasoning can be an argument which includes at least six parts, three of which are necessary for all argument whether stated or implied. These parts are: the *data* (support), the *claim,* the *warrant,* the *support* for the warrant, the *reservations,* and the *qualifier.* Figure 5-2 shows how these parts of an argument are related to each other. Examine it carefully; then examine the way each part is defined.

1. *The claim.* The idea, or conclusion a speaker wants an audience to understand and/or accept.

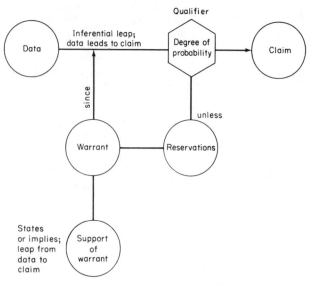

Figure 5–2.

2. *The data.* The supporting material observed and collected by the speaker to serve as evidence an audience can understand and accept as a basis for the speaker's claim. Three kinds of support may be used by a speaker:

   a. *Authoritative.* Support derived from an authority to be understood and accepted by the audience

   b. *Motivative.* Support derived from basic needs which can lead an audience through the speakers' use of motivating appeals

   c. *Substantive.* Support derived from external facts available to the speaker and which also make sense to the audience

3. *The warrant.* The part of a line of reasoning which states or implies an inference or leap from the data to the claim. The warrant allows for this inferential leap. It is a *general belief*

in the human mind, as contrasted with the data, which are specific. The warrant can also be divided into three types:

a. *Authoritative.* Belief derived from an authority to be understood and accepted by the audience

b. *Motivative.* Belief derived from emotions and motives which can be understood and accepted by the audience

c. *Substantive.* Belief derived from the relationship among external facts available to the audience

Michael and Judie Burgoon summarize the three major parts of an explanation or argument by declaring that a *claim* states what a speaker wants the audience to do; the *data* are specific beliefs and attitudes about the existence of objects or events; and a *warrant* is a general belief or attitude which justifies acceptance of the claim.[3]

Support or beliefs which are authoritative refer to ethos and credibility, treated in chapter 2 of this book. These are beliefs in which the source of the support or belief appears to have:

1. A great deal of integrity, or
2. a great deal of expertise, or
3. power, or
4. charisma.

Needs, which are motivative both in relationship to the data and the warrant, can be summarized within the scope of four kinds of needs centered in the communicators:

1. *Intrapersonal* (self-satisfaction and personal fulfillment, peace of mind); or
2. *physical* (good health, food, shelter, sexual adjustment, outward comfort); or
3. *interpersonal* (love, acceptance, belonging, status approval); or
4. *task-centered* (accomplishment, solutions to problems, removal of obstacles, meaningful work).

A person who fulfills these needs can preserve and enhance the ego, or sense of self-esteem, and can maintain personal survival as well as the survival of significant others cherished by the self. A person can also work for the maintenance of the part of society in which she or he lives.

Finally, data or warrant in relation to substantive support or beliefs can be summarized by examining at least four types of facts which provide a description of the base for these beliefs in communicators:

1. Observed phenomenon or phenomena; or
2. observed objects or events; or
3. observed behavior in a person or persons; or
4. direct factual record.

In addition to the data, warrant, and claim in a line of reasoning, there are three very important supporting parts. These may or may not seem to be present to a listener during a speech. The parts are support for the warrant, the reservations, and the qualifier.

> *Support for the warrant.* Information which provides "backing," "truth," or certification to the belief expressed in the warrant
> *Reservations.* Information directed at the claim, which recognizes certain conditions under which the claim may not be fully understood and/or acceptable to the audience
> *Qualifier.* The degree of understanding or probability the speaker aims to create within the audience (degree of cogency; review Fig. 5-1 again)

Mudd and Sillars[4] provide clear examples of the use of Toulmin's ideas for reasoning in public speech communications:

> We can expect an audience to accept a claim only when that claim is adequately justified. This means the data must be sound and the warrant must be relevant. But, as we have said, one characteristic of arguments used in rhetoric is the omission of certain elements when the arguments are delivered.
>
> Here's an example: In the wintry early months of 1974, there was considerable concern over a much discussed shortage of gasoline, one aspect of the energy crisis that bothered the greater part of the whole world. Often debated was the

proposal to ration gasoline in much the same way it was rationed during World War II. One basic argument said: "We have a shortage of gasoline and that means we're going to have to institute a system of rationing." Even when an argument is phrased in this shortened form, it needs to be organized in the mind of a listener if it is to be assessed. That is to say, listeners will supply in their own minds whatever omitted data or warrant may be needed to make the argument operate *as if it were analytical.* They do this just as they supply the missing premises needed to put Aristotelian enthymemes into syllogistic form. In this case, a warrant has to be supplied, as shown in the following layout.

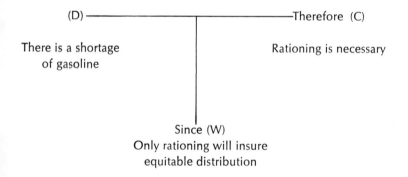

Figure 5–3.

Surely, no one will call this argument *valid* in a technical, formal sense. Nonetheless, it is clearly reasonable. In order to analyze such an argument, Toulmin requires the use of three additional concepts in his model. All three of them point to the probabilistic nature of the argument. There is *backing* (B) to support the warrant, to show that (W) *is* relevant to the case at hand; there is a *rebuttal* (R) to designate circumstances under which the warrant would *not* be applicable, and there is a *qualifier* (Q) to indicate the probabilistic quality of the claim. Now add these to the argument in our example.

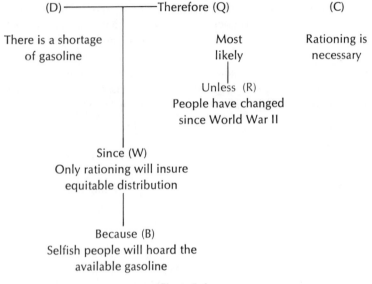

(D) ——————Therefore (Q)   (C)

There is a shortage   Most   Rationing is
of gasoline   likely   necessary

Unless (R)
People have changed
since World War II

Since (W)
Only rationing will insure
equitable distribution

Because (B)
Selfish people will hoard the
available gasoline

Figure 5–4.

One further step in the development of this argument is not mentioned by Toulmin and is not an element in his model. This step is the addition of some reasonable backing or support for the data (see Fig. 5–5).

Arguments are expected to be logical and this is the way their logicality can be tested in the mind of a listener: to organize the data in the form of a layout, to judge the truth of the data, to determine the relevance of the warrant, and to evaluate the backing for the data and the warrant and consider a possible rebuttal. On the basis of this kind of evaluation, the decision will be made whether to accept or reject the claim.

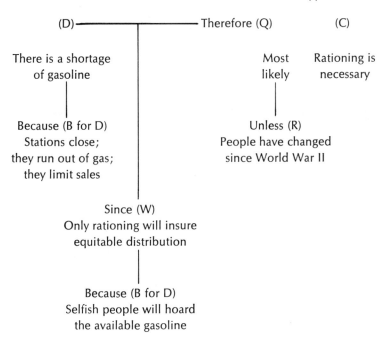

Figure 5–5.

Because we can expect this critical behavior on the part of our listeners, we will want to lay out our arguments in advance; evaluate the data, warrants, and backing, and identify rebuttal conditions and the qualifier in accordance with Toulmin's model *and in the light of your audience analysis.* We do not know any better way to formulate rhetorically effective arguments.

Whether or not the argument is sound, accurate, and influential depends on how it meets an essential test of reasoning which takes into account the speaker's choice of ideas and information and the pathways to the audience's minds. One essential test of reasoning has been offered in six basic questions for checking and testing reasoning.

These questions provide a sound guide for designing propositions and contentions for effective rhetorical speech communication. They raise six key questions we can use in practical reasoning for public communication:

1. Is the evidence sufficient?
2. Are the data sufficient, relevant, and significant enough to be accepted by the audience?
3. What kinds of warrant exist to draw any claim? Will the audience allow this warrant as a basis for an inferential claim?
4. Does the claim seem most reasonable, clear, and probable in terms of the data, warrant, and the specific purpose in communicating?
5. Does the warrant require support to make the intended point?
6. What, if any, significant reservations, rebuttal, or exceptions exist which might affect the pointedness of the line of reasoning to establish the claim?
7. All things considered, what seems to be the degree of reasonableness, understanding, and probability which the audience will arrive at in their thinking?

We must always keep in mind that the attitudes, beliefs, and values of the audience are extremely important in the speaker's choices when providing reasoning for public communication. Thus, these questions should be carefully used in constructing lines of reasoning aimed at gaining maximum effect. The task involves a great deal of effort and careful judgment, but it is worthwhile in meeting the challenge of the audience.

At the end of chapter 6 you will find a speech by Gloria Steinem and another by Leonard Woodcock. You will be asked to use the Toulmin approach and apply it to these speeches. Analyzing and diagramming is both tough and tedious, but it can be exciting. There does not seem to be any better way to formulate effective arguments than to develop and test reasoning, whether controversial or noncontroversial, which is crucial to sound and satisfying communication.

Organization Is a Key to Effective Communication

The way in which a speaker chooses to organize, or arrange, ideas in a speech helps the audience to understand the thoughts and images used by the speaker. People find meaning in organization. This idea is as old as the teaching of communication and as fresh as current research, which seeks to define and validate the role and impact of organization and the effect of the speech on an audience. When the earliest teachers of speech communication began to develop principles for communication they gave considerable importance to organization of ideas.

Traditional rhetorical theory is centered in five parts of a speech, each with its own system of organization. For example, *invention* is concerned with the discovery of information, such as an exploration of subject matter, determining key issues, and establishing proofs for the speaker's lines of reasoning; *arrangement* concerns the organization of ideas within a speech; *style* deals with the use of effective and appropriate language suitable to the speaker, the occasion, and the audience; *delivery* focuses on the best use of the voice and the body in generating meaning; and *memory* is committing the speech, once completely constructed, to memory so that the speaker can operate without notes. The last part is seldom taught today for reasons mentioned in chapter 1. If a speaker were to follow carefully all the principles in this detailed system of speechcraft, he or she would probably be effective. We should note that *one major part* of the traditional principles for effective speaking dealt exclusively with organization.

The organization of ideas in public speaking is the placement of lines of reason and supporting material in a sequence or structure which seems most rational and appealing to both speaker and listener. In addition, the speaker designs an introduction and a conclusion for the speech, which also work to increase effectiveness.

To organize a message one must select a format and pattern which is best suited for the fulfillment of a specific purpose—the precise response desired from the audience. A number of optional patterns are available. Perhaps most practical are these six:

1. the chronological pattern
2. the spatial pattern
3. the structure-function pattern
4. the topical pattern
5. the cause-effect pattern
6. the problem-solution pattern

Let us take a concise look at each of these patterns. In the *chronological*, a speech is organized according to an accurate historical or time sequence. For example, a speaker whose aim is exposition can convince the audience that the struggle for human rights in the United States is as old as the nation itself. All the lines of reason can be arranged according to events as they occurred over periods of time since the birth of the nation.

The *spatial pattern* requires the speaker to arrange ideas so that they move from the relationship of an object, place, person, or event, to another object, place, person, or event according to *spatial locations*. A speaker whose general objective is the adoption of marketing strategies for his company's new product may arrange his ideas by beginning with promotion and sales in the eastern part of the country and moving west, or in the northern part and moving south. Beginning in one region and progressing to another seems clearer for both speaker and audience than generalizing and moving in and out of regions rather haphazardly.

In speeches organized according to the *structure-function* pattern the speaker first describes the structure of an entity or phenomenon and then the ways in which this entity or phenomenon functions. For example, a speaker whose general objective at a new-employee training meeting is continuance of effective management may explain the importance of being able to conceptualize the organization's structure and then how it functions. This pattern helps the listener to understand even complex ideas with maximum clarity.

In the *topical pattern* information is categorized under topics which are directly aimed at the achievement of a specific purpose. The lines of reason are placed in categories, and are then arranged under topics in a priority, or hierarchy, of importance. The speaker treats first one and then another topic in an orderly fashion.

A speaker whose general objective was pleasure sought to create within her audience warm, good, and humorous feelings on the subject of children spending their first week in preschool. She chose the four most unusual topics she could think of and arranged them in a hierarchy leading from slightly to highly humorous by estimating how the audience would respond.

The *cause-effect* pattern of organization first focuses on the cause of some phenomenon, experience, or problem, and then moves to the effects which result. The speaker can reverse this order so that effects are described before what appear to be causes are discussed. One talks about causes and effects as they directly relate to each other and in a way which seems best suited for gaining the desired goal in an audience.

Speaking about why he felt the university faculty had called for his resignation, the president of the university, who sought to *deter* further efforts to unseat him, spoke of the various ideas he felt were largely the cause of discontent among the faculty. Then he discussed the effects, which included several faculty meetings, the drafting of a statement, a press conference to release the statement to the news media, and finally the sending of the call for resignation to the president and the board of trustees.

The *problem-solution pattern* for speech organization moves from examination of a problem to a particular solution. It can be said to move from the need to remedy a situation to a satisfying way to eliminate this need.

A political speaker wanted to reverse the trend toward what he saw as liberal and undesirable practices in the city's educational system. He also wanted to substitute policies he thought were conservatively sound. He campaigned vigorously, using one major speech which was organized on the problem-solution format. This is a common and practical way to arrange speeches when the general objective is adoption. A speaker may deal only with the problem, waiting until later speaking opportunities to propose solutions. Or, if the audience is well aware of the problem, the speaker may spend all of the time arguing a solution.

How do we know which pattern is the one to choose? Having

determined the subject, the general objective, and the specific purpose of a speech; having completed a realistic audience analysis; having engaged in careful research and reasoning; the speaker can then look at the options for organization and make a decision about which will probably hit the target—the audience. An effective introduction and conclusion to the speech will be very helpful as will referring to some basic models or organizations which have already been proven effective with audiences. Effectiveness and results should determine the pattern.

Speakers must be able to construct an outline of the information in a speech in a careful, sound, and accurate way, and then transfer this information to note cards. Therefore, the rest of this chapter is devoted to these matters.

An Effective Introduction

The introduction of a speech should accomplish four things: gain the complete attention of the audience, help to establish the speaker's ethos or credibility, foster the audience's identification with the subject, and offer the audience a forecast. The initial summary includes a statement of the proposition, or main point, and a review of the contentions in support of the main point.

An audience is more apt to focus attention on a speech if the speaker creates a strong identification for the audience with the subject. Wouldn't you be impressed by, or willing to listen to, a commentator who is apparently ego-involved with the topic by virtue of genuine interest, experience, or expertise? An obvious advantage for the speech communication class is that an ego-involved student is not going to sound matter-of-fact.

A state of readiness can be gained through the use of an initial statement. A summary of what is to be said is not an absolute necessity, but in a majority of instances it may be of value.

Perhaps the most important function of the introduction is to gain the audience's attention. There are a number of very useful ways to do this. The most frequently used are probably these six:

1. warm, personal greeting to the audience

2. a startling declaration
3. a dramatic, detailed illustration
4. a thought-provoking, pertinent quotation
5. humor in good taste, and also pertinent
6. a rhetorical question

The speaker can choose any one or even two ways to gain the audience's attention, but the introduction is most effective when it remains brief. We must remember that we are likely to weaken the effect of a speech if care and good judgment are not used in designing the introduction. A good introduction can add to our ethos and credibility with an audience and lead them into the heart of the message.

An Effective Conclusion

Summaries have been used for thousands of years, but recent research raises pertinent questions about their necessity. There is an old saying: "Tell your audience what you are going to say, say it, and then remind them of what you have said." This is an oversimplification which dramatizes the use of summaries in a message. The research which indicates that in some instances summaries are not necessary also sees other factors as providing adequate comprehension of the message by the audience. Speakers must judge for themselves, but if an audience is not familiar with the content of a message, and if the message is of considerable length, a summary can reinforce the specific message of the communicator.

The conclusion of a message is basic to the achievement of the communicator's desired goal. It provides reinforcement of the proposition or main point which was offered to the audience. It centers the audience's attention on the main point; and it conveys an attitude of completeness, a sense of being finished for the time being. There are at least six options the communicator may select to convey this completeness:

1. a challenge for the audience to think, decide, and act
2. a dramatic, detailed illustration

3. a closing and attractive quotation conveying completeness
4. a rhetorical question
5. a warm, personal farewell
6. humor in good taste and highly pertinent

The speaker and the speech do not stop abruptly. The audience should be treated to a smooth and thoughtful conclusion, whether it is invited to act enthusiastically or to ponder quietly.

Three Models for Organizing a Speech

We have given detailed consideration to the search for and selection of ideas and supporting information for a speech. We have also discussed the value of ordering ideas in public speaking. Perhaps the best practical guide for organizing ideas are some basic models from both traditional and contemporary research. The three diagrammed models given here have been used with success by thousands of students. Figure 5–6 is the General Model of Organization,[5] which pulls together all of the essential elements of a six-minute speech. It can be used for speeches of any length. Its importance lies in the way it shows the components and basic relationships which make a speech coherent and cogent. Study the diagram carefully. The introduction at the top of the diagram, includes attention-getting material, the main idea (stated as a proposition), and an initial summary. This last serves as a basic introduction to the subordinate points in support of the proposition, and it offers preliminary orientation for the audience for what is to come as the speech is being delivered. The model includes three subpoints in support of the proposition. A smooth transition is required to move from one to another. Each subordinate point contains a contention of the speaker and the necessary evidence to support the contention. All of these are supportive of the proposition (both transitions and support are marked by arrows). The speaker makes a smooth transition to the conclusion of the speech, which begins with a final summary, one that reviews and supports each subpoint and reinforces the main ideas of the speech. The speaker then provides closure, or a sense of completeness, to the

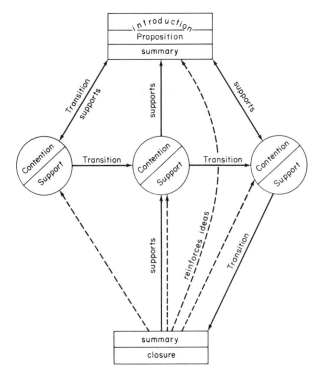

Figure 5–6. General model of organization.

speech. Notice how every component of the speech fits together so that ideas and information are not just floating aimlessly.

The second model of communication views the basic format for a speech in the form of a basic list of important items which should be a part of nearly all public speeches. It can be used as a checklist to see if a speech is structured in a thorough, logical, and organized way. On the left side of the list are items for any speech, while on the right are questions keyed specifically to the problem-solution format.[6] Study the model carefully and make use of it in speech preparation.

Suggested Format for Order in a Message

Introduction	(Gain interest
Gain attention	and attention)
Create interest	
Communicate personal involvement (ego)	
Body	(Is there a need?
Proposition or main point	A problem?
Initial summary (subordinate ideas)	What will elimi-
Detailed development of subordinate	nate it? What
ideas, with supporting material	advantages can
(data), and arranged in one of the	be evident?)
varieties of sequences	
Conclusion	(How to act?
Reinforce the specific purpose	When to act?
Challenge the receiver's thought	Where to act?)

Figure 5–7.

The third model of organization is quite detailed and includes all of the essential elements for a sound and well-structured public speech. The model shows the relationship between these key factors:[7] the components for the introduction, the body, and the conclusion of a speech; the options for an introduction and a conclusion; and the basic optional patterns for organizing the body of a speech.

The model also draws attention to the importance of developing units within the speech, each having its proper place. Transitions are required between units and supporting material, for subordinate points support the main point of the speech. Study this model carefully and refer to it as often as necessary to ensure that speeches are structured for maximum effect.

Speech construction requires us to prepare outlines, for to proceed from the main idea a speaker must have a definite plan in mind. This plan is structured in outline form.

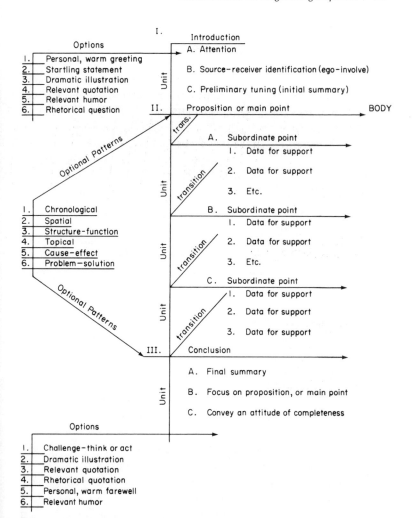

Figure 5–8. Model for developing the organization of a message.

Preparing an Outline

An outline keeps a speaker on target and ensures that everything intended to be included in the message has been said with maximum effectiveness. A detailed outline can be easily prepared once a speaker has all the information structured carefully. But detailed or not, most listeners agree that they would prefer to hear an interesting communicator speak in an orderly fashion from an outline and notes and not read from a manuscript or ramble endlessly. Few people untrained in oral interpretation or manuscript delivery can read aloud with sustained meaning. Not many people can speak for any length of time in an impromptu fashion without wandering. For most us, the safe bet in public speaking is the use of a thorough outline or notes from an outline.

There are two kinds of outline: *full-content* outline or a key-word outline. The *full-content* is a detailed outline including all of the information to be presented. Each idea, with its supporting data, is expressed in a complete sentence. The speaker can develop an overall guide to be laid out, checked, and changed until the lines of reason and the support are in an order the speaker believes is highly suited to the audience. Once a full-content outline is complete, it is not uncommon for a speaker to rework information, or seek additional information, or delete information in an effort to construct the strongest possible speech.

The *key-word outline* can be developed from a full-content outline; it omits the detail. The speaker, having the detail well prepared, uses abbreviated words and sentences to make up a condensed outline for the actual presentation. The most frequent problem to occur in classes of speech communication is that student speakers are not acquainted with full-content outlines or simply avoid making them. They prepare incomplete outlines which contribute to unorganized speeches which lack balance and the proper emphases necessary for effective communication. *Effective speaking is more likely to occur when we have developed well-constructed audience-oriented outlines than when we have not.*

Units of Ideas. An outline is made up of units of ideas which comprise the introduction, body, and conclusion of the speech. A unit contains one idea and the necessary supporting material. Units support the general goal and the specific purpose of the speech.

The units are the ideas a speaker wants an audience to remember for practical purposes and perhaps to share with others who were not in the audience. These ideas—if remembered, understood, and believed by the audience—should lead them to the specific purpose sought by the speaker.

Supporting material concerns us here only as it relates to points in an outline. A pattern must be established to organize materials effectively in achieving the desired listener response. The speaker selects information and lines of reason to support a main idea. These are *subordinate ideas*, and they must have evidence if a message is to be thorough and convincing.

An effective pattern of main and subordinate ideas should follow these four guidelines:

1. Each unit in the outline should contain one idea.
2. Less important ideas in the outline should be subordinate to more important ideas.
3. The logical relationship between units of the outline should be shown by proper indentation.
4. A consistent set of symbols should be used throughout the outline.

Two sample outlines are given below. Each was used by a speaker in a basic course in public speaking. Examine, analyze, and criticize them as a test of your knowledge about outlines. Study the information in terms of reasoning and support.

PLAYING THE MARKET: A NEW PERSONAL INTEREST

    I. Recently I've developed an interest I want to share with you.
       A. Listen first to Janet Low, who wrote *Understanding the Stock Market*. ". . . one way of helping to make the future a nice place may be to put some of today's money to work in the hope of enjoying tomorrow some of the necessities, comforts and luxuries that money can buy. In other words to buy securities."
       B. That's basically why I've dabbled in the market.

    II. I have purchased some stock for varying reasons and the results have been mediocre.

        A. First I'll mention why and how I got stock originally, second the results of my purchase, and third what I plan to do with it now.

            1. This is my first piece of stock, fifteen shares of American Motors.

            a. It cost $140, which includes the commission and one-eighth more per share for odd lot.

            b. I had gotten a tip on it and bought by calling my father's broker.

            c. Then over a couple more years I shot more money into stock, mostly on impulse, i.e., I.H., Pan Am, etc.

            2. But the result of buying stock has been a learning experience.

            a. That is, I've learned a lot by losing more than half of the money I invested.

            b. I've just accepted the fact that the money is gone for now, since there's not much I can do about it.

            c. Now stock is a pastime.

            3. Further I now can plan on what to do with the stock.

            a. I don't anticipate buying any more stock, especially low-quality stock.

            b. I'm hoping I'll be able to eventually recoup my losses.

    III. A. And so I first entered the market on a whim and a tip.

        B. The results have been unfavorable momentarily but favorable for just the experience.

        C. I plan no further market activity and hope that as the original quote indicated, I'll be able to gain some benefits and maybe retire at 25.

SELF-WORTH—A PERSONAL PERSPECTIVE

    I. I don't believe individuals value themselves much any more.

        A. Recently we saw people flock to and form long lines to fill theaters to see a girl who almost loses herself possessed by the devil in *The Exorcist*.

        B. On the other hand, organizations such as Campus Crusade for Christ will seek to get individuals to commit themselves to a *life-style* which asks them to put a savior from demonic forces into the driver's seat in their lives.

        C. Ideologically, Communists ask party members to give themselves to a collective state; economically, we live in a credit-card country where people daily turn their lives into indebtedness to bills (they are slaves to their plastic cards); academically, many of you are asked to give yourselves to exhausting study, subsequently a profession.

II. I am painfully coming to realize that one thing I *value,* it's essential to my survival, is "me."
   A. Selfish some might say? Not in the least.
   B. From the *deepest* level of consciousness to the surface levels most obvious to me, what I am coming to value most is *me*— What is a value?
   C. A *value* is a *standard* for approaching and avoiding things or events in life.
      1. It is a *psychological anchor* built into a system of values deep within persons.
      2. According to communication theorists Redding and Steele, values are concepts of the good in us.
      3. Milton Rokeach, writing in his book *The Nature of Human Values* (1973), says: "A value is an enduring belief that a specific mode of conduct or end-state of existence is personally or socially preferable to an opposite or converse mode of conduct or end-state of existence."
         and
      4. These definitions of value are then relevant to preserving and letting grow—"me."

With these descriptions of *value* in mind
   D. Let's see what I mean—
      1. Anchored deep within me is an enduring belief that I must act, *even at the expense of upsetting others,* to take care of my own self—this is a tremendous concept of something good to ponder.
      2. But, some of you might ask, can you illustrate more carefully what you mean? I can.

III. One can see how I value me by looking at some views that express my feeling.
   A. The "me" I treasure becomes of apparent value when I feel others are making such overwhelming demands that I feel all chopped up:
      1. Thus I can identify in these situations with the words from *Jesus Christ Superstar* when the figure of Jesus was being overwhelmed by the sick and afflicted and he cried out in shrieking tones—Heal yourselves! . . . Everyone wanted a piece of him.
   B. The "me" I treasure becomes of apparent value when *myself*

gets caught up in a *success-motivated* "rat race" of social-professional demands which can engulf me.

    1. I find my *center* in reviewing the words of Henry David Thoreau: "Why should we be in such desperate haste to succeed, and in such desperate enterprises? If a man does not keep pace with his companions, perhaps it's because he hears a different drummer. Let him step to the music he hears, however measured or far away."

C. The "me" I treasure becomes apparent when others think they should *take charge* of me; that I must strive to live up to their expectations regardless.

    1. I am strengthened by the Gestalt prayer of Fritz Perles: "I do my thing and you do your thing. I am not in this world to live up to your expectations, and you are not in this world to live up to mine. You are you and I am I. And if by chance we find each other—it's beautiful. If not, it can't be helped."

D. The "me" I treasure becomes apparent when I act in a way in which I am *not true* to myself, and I remember from *Hamlet,* Polonius' advice to his son Laertes, who was about to depart for a long journey:

    1. "To thine ownself be true, and it must follow, as the night the day, thou canst not then be false to any man."

E. Along with these views perhaps I remember a scriptual lesson which queries: "What does it profit a man if he gains the world and loses himself?"

IV. What does all this add up to?

A. I must take care of "me" and treasure "me" deeply.

B. People may ask too much. I may lose sight of me, and others' expectations can be exhausting—yet I must not get lost—lose me!

C. The feeling *for me* I have seen summed up in the title of a favorite book of mine by Jess Lair, *I Ain't Much Baby but I'm All I Got.*

SUMMARY

This chapter is focused on reasoning and the organization of ideas in the speech. A message with accuracy and integrity requires sound reasoning and organization in the presentation of ideas. Reasoning is the process of using known or believed information to explain or prove other statements less well understood or accepted.

Statements may or may not be controversial in public speaking. Whether one seeks to persuade or only explain, a speaker must reason with an audience.

Reasoning in speaking with an audience involves developing carefully worded statements drawn from a speaker's ideas and support from research. The speaker can construct sound contentions in support of a proposition with the aim of achieving a specific purpose with an audience. One of the most practical ways to improve one's reasoning is the Toulmin approach. According to this approach, an argument or line of reasoning possesses at least the data, the claim, the warrant, the support for the warrant, the reservations, and the qualifier. We can test our reasoning or that of another by looking at the parts of an argument and subjecting them to the probing questions included in this chapter. The approach to reasoning offered here is of little or no value to the speaker who only reads about it; it must be applied to be useful! The result can be sound, accurate, and influential reasoning.

Organization, along with effective reasoning, is a key to success in speaking with an audience. One needs to arrange ideas logically in order to achieve the precise response sought from an audience. Six patterns of organization offer the speaker practical options: the chronological, the spatial, the structure-function, the topical, the cause-effect, and the problem-solution. The speaker can also choose from at least six ways of gaining the audience's attention, and six ways of achieving closure. As a practical guide for the organization of ideas, the chapter includes three models of organization which have proven to be highly effecitve.

A procedure which is often difficult for the student of public speaking is constructing an outline. However, outlining is a valuable procedure in reasoning and arranging ideas for a speech. The value of outlining is detailed here and is bound into two sample outlines.

The speech ultimately becomes the spoken word, and words are a major concern in the expression of ideas. Therefore, the final chapter is devoted to words and the uses or misuses of language in speech.

NOTES

1. Carroll C. Arnold, *Criticism of Oral Rhetoric* (Columbus: Charles E. Merrill, 1974), p. 48.
2. Stephen Toulmin, *The Uses of Argument* (Cambridge: At the University Press, 1958).
3. Michael Burgoon and Judie K. Burgoon, "Message Strategies in Influence Attempts," in *Communication and Behavior,* ed. Gerhard J. Hanneman and William J. McEven (Reading: Addison-Wesley, 1975), pp. 149–65.
4. Charles S. Mudd and Malcolm Sillars, *Speech: Content and Communication,* 3rd ed. (New York: Thomas Y. Crowell Company, 1975), pp. 167–69. Reprinted with permission from the publisher.
5. This model was introduced to our students by James R. Seward while he was associate director of "The Communication of Ideas and Attitudes."
6. John J. Makay and William R. Brown, *The Rhetorical Dialogue: Contemporary Concepts and Cases* (Dubuque: William C. Brown, 1972), p. 233. Reprinted with permission from the publisher.
7. John J. Makay and Thomas C. Sawyer, *Speech Communication Now! An Introduction to Rhetorical Influences* (Columbus: Charles E. Merrill, 1973), p. 162. Reprinted with permission from the publisher.

CHAPTER 6

THE USE OF WORDS FOR
INTENDED MEANING

Many of the most memorable moments of an entire era or generation may be called to mind with a single collection of words. This is
true of the history of a people or of a person. The American people
have enshrined some of the important words of the revolution that
won their independence in monuments at their capital, Washington,
D.C., in order to commemorate these great moments in the nation's
life. To recall those times we read the words of those who dreamed
dreams, the words of those who died with the dreams on their lips.
Think of the familiar refrain of Hale's death proclamation: "I only
regret that I have but one life to lose for my country." Or Paine's:
"These are the times that try men's souls." Or Henry's: "Give me
liberty, or give me death!" In war, in peace, in strife, in courage, in
pride, and in shame, it is our words that mark the life we share. With
the words "We, the people . . .," an independent people was pro-
claimed.

Words inspire nations and individuals. Moments in our lives can be held in a select place in our memories by the words that were used. These moments may be recollected vividly and realistically by recalling the words of the moment. Sorrows and joys are kept in thought and mind with words. We think of the special times when someone says, "Remember when . . ." Or "This is like the time when . . ." In a sense, we are defined by words that describe or were used to express deep feelings or experiences. In childhood and in age, we keep the words for special times in a place apart, so that in saying or hearing them we call forth a part of ourselves.

Words stand for or represent us when we say to a friend: "I give you my word." The friend is to understand that if we can be believed or trusted, then our word is legitimate and valuable. To give one's word is a promise of credibility.

Language is very much a part of our personal credibility, but so many times we take this for granted. Words form an important part of the world in which we live. We have all experienced words that just did not fit a situation or did not adequately describe an experience.

We learn that words can be used for many purposes. Perhaps it's a sign of the times in which we live, but frequently words are viewed in light of the adage that "talk is cheap." Many have grown to distrust words. It is not surprising that some persons would abuse a vehicle as valuable and useful as language. Although most language is genuinely shared, some use it in a counterfeit manner. This may produce some initial gains for individuals; but the ultimate end is the denigration of language, which is a loss to all.

It should be clear that the public speaker has some special and unique responsibilities in the use of language, for he or she should be keenly aware of the power, utility, and meaning of language in communicating with others. The speaker has a special responsibility for being aware of the uses and abuses of language.

In this chapter we will examine the speaker's use of language, and ask several important questions: What difference does it make in what way a speaker uses language? How do words have meaning? Should the speaker be conscious of the words he or she uses? Are the words that a speaker uses important enough to make a difference in whether or not the speaker's goal is adopted?

Language: Word-Thought-Thing

Speakers communicate the substance of their thoughts with words, which are symbols used to represent life experience.

> Language has meaning because it is symbolic. It represents, or refers to something other than itself. It is by this symbolizing, representation, and reference that words which compose a language come to mean. Likewise, a word is a symbol of something. The something to which a word points or generates thought about is called a referent. It is important to note here that we are not just concerned with two notions —those of symbol and referent—but also of thought.[1]

Symbol-referent-thought is illustrated by the "semantic triangle," originally designed by I. A. Richards and C. K. Ogden.

The triangle shows that there is not an absolute relationship between a symbol or word and the referent or thing. The relation-

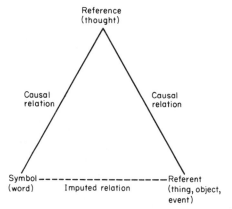

Figure 6–1. The semantic triangle. From C. K. Ogden and I. A. Richards "Meaning of Meaning." (Harcourt, Brace Jovanovich, 1923), p. 11.

ship is drawn by the receiver of the symbol. If the connection between the word and the thing is sufficient, a word may have meaning, but even when the relationship is established, there is no guarantee that it is the same from person to person. The word (symbol) may cause a thought, which in turn is attached to a thing, object, or event (referent); but again there can be no assurance that words mean exactly the same thing for each person.

Study the triangle for several moments. Then try seeing its principle by focusing on an object and labeling it. Picture an abstraction, such as freedom, and assign meaning to it.

An interesting test of the semantic triangle can be taken with "free association," a technique used by psychoanalysts, in which a stimulus word is pronounced and the response is the first word that comes to the mind of the client. On a typical word-association test, responses will cluster in fairly predictable ways. There may be three or four words that persons normally associate with the stimulus word and there may be an additional five or six words that are typical responses; but there will be any number of word responses which are totally unique. For example, if we were to ask 500 people what word they associate with book, we would probably receive a high number of responses like paperback, page, shelf, or chapter. But we would also receive many unique responses, such as brain, see, or automobile. The unique responses show that any number of things may be called to mind when a speaker uses a word. There will certainly be a fairly common response or a typical response, as we have seen, but there will also be a number of unique responses.

This is particularly true when a word is in everyday use. The more a word is used, the greater the chances that it will have several different meanings. In cases where a word has several meanings and the audience cannot easily and quickly affix a meaning to the words, ambiguity may result. If the speaker utters an ambiguous sentence and does not realize it, he or she may continue speaking while the minds of the audience are left behind, trying to figure out what has been said.

For example, suppose a speaker is talking about preventing cruelty to animals. The speaker says something like: "The killing of the trappers really saddens me." At first the listener is confused. Did the speaker take the law into his own hands and do the trappers in, or is the speaker saddened by the actions of the trappers who are killing animals? This kind of confusion can be straightened out by the context in which a statement is made, but if the speaker leaves the matter unclear the audience will not understand.

A much more common mistake is to use a pronoun without a specific referent. "He said that it was going to be all right if they could get it fixed in time for him." An audience may be tied into mental knots after listening to this kind of language. It is very frustrating to be left in the dark by words that have no clear referent. If the speaker is oblivious to the audience's frustration, he or she may expect some hostility from the audience.

Again, the semantic triangle demonstrates that there is not a direct or immediate relation between the symbol and the referent. The only relation the symbol, or word, has with the referent is that which we give it. Let us consider the word *revolution*. If we put the word in a political context, what thoughts are raised? What meanings are generated? The results may be quite different from person to person. The person who uses the word may even have a unique meaning in mind.

If the president of the United States in a television address says: "It's time for a new American Revolution in this country!" the meaning would be quite different from the same statement uttered by the president of an extremist political organization. There is nothing automatic about words and meaning, which can be unique to each individual mind.

> We must remember that the only reason certain words seem "proper" in referring to things is that we have agreed to use them in that way. . . . people will argue interminably over the symbols "democracy," "religion," "love," or even "interpersonal communication," believing there is only one true meaning of a term. . . . because a symbol exists there is no guarantee that something "out there" to which it refers exists. In addition, there is only the slightest possibility that every-

one thinks about the same referent when a particular symbol is used.[2]

The use of a symbol is an invitation to respond. Language is such an invitation. When speakers address an audience, they should be aware that many of the responses the language evokes will be unique, not at all what they expected. It is necessary to be as clear and straightforward with language as possible.

Statements Invite Responses

Statement-making by speakers invites audience response. However, speakers need to be cautious about their choice of words—will they elicit the specific response wanted from an audience?

A student was arguing for the adoption of a plan to reduce welfare costs in the United States. Part of the problem and the solution described in the speech centered around children born out of wedlock and their subsequent dependence on county welfare. Every time the student spoke of these children he referred to them as *bastards,* and each reference brought about nonverbal cues of discomfort from the audience. The speaker sought a favorable response to his plan. His statements about "unnecessary bastards born in Franklin County" brought about the reverse effect. Most of the audience let him know the resentment he had created. One man's view sums up this response: "At one time 'bastard' may have been an acceptable term for a baby born to unmarried parents. I've been around, including three years in the army. I am also an adopted person. 'Bastard' today is a negative, profane word to most people, and I was so upset at your use of it in the context of your speech I could hear nothing else."

A young woman in the same class told her audience, "I have discovered all of you have been around persons using marijuana and about half have tried it at least once. There are only three persons here who regularly smoke. The issue I believe we must all face is whether or not the frequent use of marijuana is likely physically and psychologically to damage the user. I don't believe it does, and I will explain to you why. First let me tell you what I mean by 'frequent use' and 'physical and psychological damage,' and then we can examine my contentions with care." In the language which followed the speaker carefully, descriptively, and vividly developed her case, so that everyone understood her view and invitation for agreement. They could weigh the evidence for themselves and the statement-making was helpful.

We Project a Self-Image through Words

Hugh Prather, writing in *Notes to Myself,* tells us:

Last night I started using swear words with Bill when I thought I was sounding nicer than I felt. Evidently I want to swear in order to become more real—or is it to sound more real? When I swear, I am being something rather than saying something. Profanity fixes the other person's attention on my words rather than my thoughts.[3]

This excerpt shows how one person reflected on his projection of *himself* through the use of a particular sort of language. Words work with appearance to project to an audience an image of the speaker created by each listener. We can try to predict what our words in public communication will project about us. We can select language with an eye toward the creation of meaning about ourselves consistent with our intended self-image.

A student spoke to a neighborhood book review group of his master's thesis in human communication. His parents were members of this group. Although his youth, his clothes, his voice and gestures, in a sense his presence, projected his image, his words probably said the most about him. He was a communication specialist who could not communicate with his audience. His use of jargon, abstract terms, and theoretical verbal orientation dominated the message. He missed the target and projected an image of a bright, well-educated, impractical person who was insensitive to and out of touch with his audience and the real world as they knew it.

A more dramatic and certainly familiar example of image projection and words can be found in Lenny Bruce. In one of the closing moments of the film *Lenny,* a film which focused on some aspects of the life of the late comedian, one especially dramatic scene took place in a courtroom. Lenny had been arrested and prosecuted a number of times for using words in his public performances which were judged to be obscene. He was about to have his cabaret license taken away, and he pleaded with the court: "Don't take away my words!" Language got Bruce into serious trouble in the 1950s and 1960s until his tragic death. Having seen and heard Bruce when he was alive, having seen Dustin Hoffman portray him in the film, and having read the book *Ladies and Gentleman—Lenny Bruce*, I can see several different *images* of the comedian based on the *words* he chose for public communication. A decade after his death, the *words* which Bruce was silenced for using were spoken in the film, and earned Hoffman an Academy Award nomination.

The plea "Don't take away my words" has special significance for public speakers, for the effect of speech communication is related directly to the *words* used. Not only do we obviously need words to speak to an audience, but we must have the ability to choose words carefully and use them meaningfully if we are to achieve specific purposes, the precise responses we seek.

Audience Adaptation and Selection of Language

Speakers who have analyzed their thoughts about a subject and goal for speaking, who have analyzed their audiences in order to adapt effectively, who have thoroughly researched, supported, reasoned, and organized a speech, and who have practiced delivering it, can still fail if the language is poor for the speaker-audience relationship. We must have essential information about language and meaning, and language and style, and use this information effectively if we are to achieve success. "Her lectures are ambiguous, dry, and I never know what she means," one student recently declared to a friend. "I know," said the friend. "I think she is up in the clouds or high in her ivory tower." Both students agreed that if it were not for the textbook used in the course they would not be learning a thing.

When the language of a speaker baffles members of the audience, the speaker's efforts are a waste. The professor who declares:

"Ninety percent of my class does not understand my words but my constituency is the other 10 percent!" makes a tragic declaration. Surely the speaker must try to reach the majority of the audience.

When we are in the developmental stages of speech preparation and have analyzed the audience, we are also in the stage of adjusting ideas to people so that people can adjust to ideas. This requires that the speaker make the language appropriate to the audience. For example, the most difficult task a communication consultant faced with a speakers bureau of physicians was to get doctors to adjust the language of their speeches for different audiences. Members of the bureau had great difficulty talking about disease and treatment plans without using technical language. Careful work on the use of language for audience adaptation proved successful, and the physicians are now speaking meaningfully to different public audiences in a large metropolitan area.

Personal and Social Meaning

It is difficult to separate persons from their words. Language is something of a trademark unique to each individual, and yet we share ideas, thoughts, and feelings within the common language. This is part of the paradox of language—it sets us apart as individuals and it serves as the basis of community life and expression. The paradox illustrates the private and public levels of meaning in our lives. Language has different meanings in various social, cultural, and situational contexts. For example, it is common practice among the Apache people to remain silent in a number of social and family settings. The family of an Apache student who has returned from college receives the child with joyful silence, which may continue for hours or even days at a time.[4] The Apache are reluctant to apply words to heartfelt emotions. Silence is a part of language as much as spoken word.

A speaker can choose to remain silent when the intended message is already in the minds of the audience, as when the audience is asked a question.

Too many times we assume that a particular meaning is conveyed with words, when in fact the audience is hearing something totally different. If we are sensitive to the possibility of a misunderstanding, then a significant part of the problem is solved. But more often than not the beginning speaker has not yet developed an awareness of the uses and misuses of language and cannot read signs from the audience that it does not understand what is meant. The worst mistake of all is to adopt an attitude about language voiced to Alice by Humpty Dumpty in Lewis Carroll's *Through the Looking Glass:*

> "When *I* use a word," Humpty Dumpty said, in rather a scornful tone, "It means just what I choose it to mean—neither more nor less."
>
> "The question is," said Alice, "whether you *can* make words mean so many different things."
>
> "The question is," said Humpty Dumpty, "which is to be master—that's all."
>
> Alice was too much puzzled to say anything . . .[5]

Many beginning speakers adopt the attitude that language and its meaning will take care of itself. This dampens the speaker's ability to communicate appropriate meanings to an audience. Language— that is, words and meanings—does not exist in a sterile environment that never changes. Language is as alive as the person who uses it. It achieves its major effectiveness as it is shared by the speaker with the audience. In this sense, language is a part of the shared experience of the speaker and the audience.

Two Primary Levels of Language Sharing

Language has two primary levels—*private* and *public*. Different meanings may exist for the speaker or the audience at each level. For example, how many times have you heard a joke or shared an experience in one setting with a particular group of friends and later, recalling this hilarious experience with someone else, gotten a blank stare? "So what's the punch line?" the person asks. You apologetically reply, "I guess you had to be there."

The speaker and the audience carry a multitude of experiences and language meanings with them. Some may be unique and private, while the majority are fairly common to all. The speaker should assess the meanings that may exist in an audience. By examining the reasons that have brought an audience together, clues to meaning for an audience can be uncovered. One would speak differently to a convention of religious leaders than to a gathering of antique enthusiasts. Both groups have private meanings which are deep and profound and significant enough to shape the involvement of each in a special interest or concern. Within each group is an interpersonal level of meaning which grows with the extent to which persons are able to give private meanings to each other. In this way new meanings are generated by the sharing experiences.

Language is very much a part of this evolution of meaning. Words are continually woven in and out between the private and public levels of language and experience sharing. Each of us carries part of the public experiences into the private level, and we may later recycle this private meaning in another public experience. Through this continuing process, new meanings and experiences are always being generated.

To understand the manner in which the private and public levels of meaning and language operate, it may be helpful to study the relationship between the two. We have observed that each level contributes to the other. In the speaking situation, speakers determine the extent to which the two levels will generate new meanings and experience for the audience and for themselves. Speakers begin with several assumptions about the audience based on their appraisal of who the audience is and why they have gathered. Speakers' appraisals are estimations of what members of the audience share in terms of meaning and experience. Through interaction with the audience speakers may *derive* a series of new experiences and meanings and may also introduce new language which describes these meanings.

For example, imagine the coach of a losing football team addressing them at half time. Each person in the locker room has private and public meanings and experiences. One player may have stepped out of bounds with the ball, and his thoughts are focused on this mistake. Another may be feeling the pain of an injury. Each has his own private thoughts and experiences to wrestle with while at the same time he understands that the team is losing the game. The coach sees a group of losers with their heads down silently justifying their individual failures and sufferings. The team expects him to say something like "You can do it gang," and give them a pep talk. The knowledge is shared and certain words are appropriate to express this meaning. But the coach knows that unless he can generate new group awareness and identity, he might as well not bother to lead the team out of the dressing room for the second half. His task as a speaker is to *derive* new group meaning for the team and bring each individual out of his private world into a *new* public level. This is only possible if he can get each individual to contribute to the new jointly created public spirit, which might help them to win the game. What can the coach do? He must draw individuals into the public level. To do this he may say something like, "Look at you. Look at you. Heads down licking your wounds. Johnson, you look like the only guy who ever stepped out of bounds with the ball in the history of this game. But as you sit over there punishing yourself, you're punishing your teammates as well. You got more to give us than your grief. Come on! Play ball! And look at you, Smith, over there nursing that arm like you are the only guy who has picked up any bruises tonight. Maybe you don't remember, but the guy who gave that to you didn't get up till a long time after you did. Come on, Smith, flex your muscle! That's it. Flex it. You see what Smith is doing?! You see?"

The coach has accomplished part of his goal; he has drawn individuals into the public level. And in doing this he has begun accomplishing the second part of his task; that is, to derive a new shared spirit on the public level. The group must share new meaning in viewing itself, partly through new shared language. The coach continues: "You know something? You don't look like losers to me. As a matter of fact, you look like you're hungry. This next half that bunch of turkeys are going to come strutting out like they own this place, but they don't know how hungry you are, do they Johnson? Isn't that right? Hey, Smith, they don't know how hungry you are, do they? Come on you guys, it's Thanksgiving." With these words a new shared spirit is developed.

Word Choice Is Crucial

The force of a speaker's language is brought to bear upon the ultimate speaking objective. We have already noticed the ability of language to elicit vivid and dramatic responses, but words may affect us in subtle and perhaps unknown ways. Words significantly govern the way we see the world. Benjamin Whorf, a man who worked most of his life as an insurance investigator, described the effect of words on our thoughts and actions.[6] In his investigations of fires Whorf noticed that the conditions which made a fire possible were reflected in the descriptions of the fires themselves. To illustrate the effects of words on the world we see, Whorf gives an account of a visit to a leather tannery warehouse which had burned. The fire produced considerable damage and financial loss. It had been caused by a fan which was blowing air across the "drying" animal hides. The fan had developed an electrical short, but was able to continue operating, so that it blew the flames onto the leather goods, which in turn caught fire.

Later, as he viewed the situation, Whorf asked: Why was it necessary to have a fan "dry" the hides by blowing air across them? Why not direct the fan out of the warehouse (thus preventing the fire hazard) and dry the hides by drawing air across the hides? In this case, word choice reflects a proposed course of action or perception of the world.

When speakers choose a word, they are also suggesting a particular way of seeing or viewing the matter in question to the audience. Words are the seeds of actions which may be urged by the speaker. Consider the differences suggested by these complementary word sets which can have the same referent: exterminate–murder, set free–cast off, save–horde, judge–condemn. The choice of words is dependent upon the speaker's way of looking at things and affects the way in which the audience views a matter.

The speaker's words may suggest a particular way of thinking or acting toward an issue, object, or person. An audience may be brought to symbolically enact an event or action through words. The speaker's words can reflect the urgency, fervency, or force of the action itself and initiate the forces to actually accomplish or prevent an action.[7]

Suppose that a speaker is presenting an argument for the adoption of a bond issue to rebuild the flood wall around a community. The speaker may have very personal and emotional feelings about this issue, which are her incentives for speaking out. She may speak in very vivid, narrative terms of the kinds of destruction a shattered flood wall might bring. The speaker's words can describe the rampant and raging torrent of water tearing through the deteriorated flood wall. This episode is symbolically re-enacted in the minds of the audience through the use of the speaker's illustrative language.

Words Express Experience

Words can convey whole worlds of experience. The acute and perceptive speaker may be able to find just a few words to summarize the feelings and thoughts of an audience. *War and Peace* is the title given by Leo Tolstoy to the collection of experiences, plot, story line, and characters which make up his epic novel. *Entitlement* names a series or conglomeration of things encompassed within one thing.[8] Sometimes a single word or collection of words become emblematic of a much more detailed phenomenon or event. In politics the political slogan may portray all that the candidate stands for; for example, Eisenhower's "I like Ike" or Truman's "The buck stops here."

Speakers may seek to reduce a complicated or detailed set of issues into a single word or phrase. Real entitlement, in its most powerful and profound senses, combines the ironic with the practical elements of reduction. The speaker draws together many strong emotions and ideas through the entitlement.

A very vivid example concerns the speaker who had experienced a tornado along with his whole community just a short time before. The tornado had literally torn its way through the city, destroying hundreds of homes, uprooting trees, and claiming lives. The speaker was trying to summarize and draw together his own and others' experiences. The speaker's home had been one of those leveled by the tornado. He concluded his comments by sharing a simple story with the audience.

The man had spoken about not being able in the past to throw anything away. The attic of his home had been filled with 25 years of memorabilia, which all seemed important—the crutches that had helped him get around when he broke his leg, the water skis that were never used after the boat had been sold ten years before, the art work of three children and all his grandchildren, thousands of bits and pieces of unused fabric. Now, because of the tornado, all of it was gone. The only thing that remained was the door frame of the house with the locked door still intact. He told his audience that as he made his way to the front of the house to view the devastation he had looked down at his feet and seen a single book opened and lying on the welcome mat. When he picked it up, he read the title in disbelief. It was *Gone with the Wind*.

The speaker used entitlement—the reduction of many diverse things into a single word or phrase—to share his experience with his audience by applying one event to a vast network of experiences. Entitlement is an important language device for the speaker.

There is a danger, however, in the use of entitlements, and that is its use in detrimental ways. Since the title of something does not *contain* the whole but *represents* or *stands for* something else, we must remember that the slogan is not the political candidate and the catchword is not the product. Speakers and listeners should study the way entitlements are used ethically.

The media critic Marshall McLuhan has observed that the media which continually bombard our senses and minds have condensed and distorted many complex ideas into mere labels. Instead of thoroughly and substantially treating an idea, its merts and demerits, we dispense labels which simply "tag" something as a plus or minus. He calls this "label libel."[9] The title of a section of a chapter in a book is empty of the detail found in each paragraph and sentence. Chapter titles give even less detail, and the book title retains the least detail. In similar fashion a speaker should see that the audience knows or is aware of the detail which lies behind or beneath an entitlement.

We have already seen that a name may serve a useful purpose for the speaker by summarizing detail, and that there are dangers in using such names when they become simply labels without any substance behind them. The application of names to things, events, or persons may prove to be a strategy in itself. In the speaking situation the speaker, by virtue of being the speaker, is in a position to initiate names for things. A name is a means of control.

It has long been a part of human psychology that the one who names is the one who has power. The speaker who applies names to things is able to shape the audience's view of the world. The way in which a speaker applies names, describes, or explains ideas to an audience affects the way the audience will react to the ideas. This may be part of the strategy the speaker adopts in the communication of ideas. Just as a chain of logic flows through a major premise, a minor premise, and a conclusion, the speaker may carefully apply a series of names to bring the audience to the desired conclusion. In effect, the language of the speaker is used to shape the manner in which the audience perceives the topic.

Note how Shakespeare's Mark Antony calls the motives and intentions of Caesar's assassins into question. He carefully leads the audience to question some of the names that were used to describe the circumstances surrounding the death of Caesar:

> The noble Brutus
> Hath told you Caesar was ambitious.
> If it were so, it was a grievous fault,
> And grievously hath Caesar answer'd it.
> Here, under leave of Brutus and the rest
> (For Brutus is an honourable man;
> So are they all, all honourable men),
> Come I to speak in Caesar's funeral.
> He was my friend, faithful and just to me;
> But Brutus says he was ambitious,
> And Brutus is an honourable man.

He hath brought many captives home to Rome,
Whose ransoms did the general coffers fill.
Did this in Caesar seem ambitious?
When that the poor have cried, Caesar hath wept;
Ambition should be made of sterner stuff.
Yet Brutus says he was ambitious;
And Brutus is an honourable man.
You all did see that on the Lupercal
I thrice presented him a kingly crown,
Which he did thrice refuse. Was this ambition?
Yet Brutus says he was ambitious;
And sure he is an honourable man.
                    (*Julius Caesar*, act 3, Scene 2)

In the lines which follow members of the crowd reason aloud and complete the chain of name questioning that Antony has begun. The audience begins to question Caesar's "ambition"—What ambition is there in a man who refuses a king's crown? What is the basis or substance of honor in the actions of Brutus and his friends? The crowd completes the questioning of the names applied to these men by equating Brutus' honor and that of his friends with treason.

The speaker's use of a name is much like a picture frame. The frame defines the vision inside itself. This may strongly affect the way we see the total picture, but if we are presented with evidence questioning the lines of the frame, the strict bounds of the picture may be broken and expanded or reduced in focus. The speaker and the language chosen controls the audience's focus.

Making Language Successful and Effective

In summarizing the importance of language to the speaker, the 10 statements below can be of considerable help. They are the result of both empirical and experimental research findings plus the observation of hundreds of speakers in recent times.

1. Know the audience and try to view the language its members may use in translating the speech.
2. Strive for accuracy, clarity, and naturalness in choosing words

to represent objects, events, things, and ideas.

3. Avoid vague and ambiguous terms which can mislead the listener.

4. Avoid sweeping generalizations, overstatement of the case, and words which seem loaded with biased emotional charges.

5. Choose words which can be vivid without distorting symbolic reality.

6. Study the speeches of others with particular attention to the way in which language is used with the intended audience; make some conclusions from this study.

7. Work to increase vocabulary and apply the increase wisely in speaking.

8. Avoid jargon and, where possible, use ordinary words that are in general use.

9. Speak as *often* as possible, each time with a primary concern for words and the way they can work.

10. Remember that *meanings* are in people, who create and assign *meaning* to symbolic referents.

SUMMARY

This chapter focuses on the use of words, as language, to create intended meaning in speaking with an audience. The importance of words in speaking and listening can be easily overlooked if we only concentrate on self-confidence, physical projection, research, reasoning, and organizing ideas. But words are central to human personality and are instrumental in the creation of understanding.

Meeting needs in choosing words essentially begins with explaining the relationship between words, thoughts, and things. Words are not things, but only *stand for* something else. A listener may, for example, understand significantly different meanings than those intended by the speaker. We also examined the notion that words in statements are actually invitations to an audience for response. If we are careless in our word choice, we may not get the precise response we want.

A speaker projects part of a self-image through words. How you look and how you sound certainly contribute a great deal to what image you project. But what words you choose to represent you and your ideas also contribute significantly to your image.

Throughout our reading, discussion, and applications we have tried to adapt to audiences. Part of this adaptive process requires the selection of words most suited to creating both interest and meaning with an audience. Because knowledge about personal and social meanings can help create both interest and meaning, kinds of meaning were described and the levels of language sharing.

Finally, we need to understand the relationship between language and the speaker's objective and words as expressions of experience. Words have a significant effect on the ways in which the speaker and the audience view the world in which they live. Ten suggestions were given to help make for effective use of words in speaking with an audience.

NOTES

1. John J. Makay and Beverly A. Gaw, *Personal and Interpersonal Communication: Dialogue with the Self and with Others* (Columbus: Charles E. Merrill, 1975), p. 82.
2. Ibid., p. 81.
3. Hugh Prather, *Notes to Myself* (Utah: Real People's Press, 1970).
4. K. H. Basso, "To Give upon Words: Silence in Western Apache Culture," in *Language and Social Context*, ed. Pier Paolo Giglioli (London: Penguin Books, 1972), pp. 67–86.
5. D. Slobin, *Psycholinguistics* (Glenview, Ill.: Scott, Foresman, 1971), p. 96.
6. Benjamin Whorf, *Language, Thought and Reality* (Cambridge: MIT Press, 1956).
7. Kenneth Burke, *Language as Symbolic Action* (Berkeley: University of California Press, 1968).
8. Kenneth Burke, *Rhetoric of Religion* (Berkeley: University of California Press, 1970).
9. Marshall McLuhan, *Understanding Media: The Extensions of Man* (New York: McGraw-Hill, 1964).

Appendix A

A SPECIAL ASSIGNMENT WITH SPEECHES

We can summarize the chapters now by completing the assignment which follows. It requires the practical application of the information we have studied about public speech communication as well.

On the following pages you will find the complete texts of two speeches. The first was delivered by Gloria Steinem, active spokesperson in the feminist movement and editor of *Ms. Magazine*. The second speech is by Leonard Woodcock, former president of the United Auto Workers.

1. Study each speech carefully. Determine the proposition for each audience and write it out. Identify each piece of supporting material and apply appropriate tests to the support. Write this information down.
2. Briefly recreate in writing the rhetorical setting for each

speech, the communicator's objectives, and each specific purpose.

3. See what you can find out generally about the speakers' delivery.

4. Write a composite about the audiences each probably faced, and include some specific suggestions you might offer the speakers about adapting to their audiences.

5. Study each speech carefully again, looking for the speaker's use of entitlements.

6. Using the Toulmin approach, analyze on paper the reasoning each speaker offers.

7. Indicate in writing the organizational structure and patterns of organization which seem evident in the speeches.

8. Construct a full-content and a key-word outline for each speech.

9. Write an essay on the language of each speech, focusing on both the style and meanings, at least as *you* perceive them.

Put all your written information together; have your instructor review it; and determine for yourself what you have learned from completing the tasks.

THE FEMINIST REVOLUTION*

A Speech by

Gloria Steinem†

I would like to talk to you, not only as advertising people, but as individual human beings who are experiencing—as we all are—the very deep and important changes that are going on now.

I'm not going to talk to you about the Equal Rights Amendment, about equal pay, about child care centers, about all the issues that I'm sure you know. I've been told that this group is a very, very well-informed one.

Instead, I would like to tell you an anthropological story—a possible explanation of history, that may very well be true, but angers patriarchal and Freudian scholars so much that it's still considered very controversial.

IN THE BEGINNING, THERE WAS A GYNECOCRACY

I would like to suggest to you that the social order we see around us now is neither the natural one, nor the only one that human beings have achieved—that for the first half of human history, it's likely that there was a gynecocracy, not a matriarchy which imitated patriarchy and came later, but a gynecocracy which meant that women were the first class citizens, that women were considered superior beings, and that they were worshipped as goddesses. In fact, we see residual women goddesses in most of the great religions.

Now, much of the reason that women were worshipped during these first 5000 years was that we bore the children. We've somehow allowed ourselves to get talked into the idea that bearing children is an inferior function—and therefore makes us inferior. But in fact, for the whole first half of human history, it was considered superior and

* An address to the Central Region Annual Meeting of the American Association of Advertising Agencies, Chicago, October 31, 1973.

† Editor, *Ms. Magazine*; active spokesperson in the Women's Movement

very much envied. It was imitated by men in their religious and tribal ceremonies.

Much of the reason for child bearing's envy and worship was its mystery. Women were thought to bear fruit like trees when they were ripe: cause and effect had not been discovered yet. Paternity had not been discovered yet.

The discovery of paternity was a very important event in the history of humankind—at least as important as how to make fire, or how to make metal. It began a change in all the social systems that were to come. The idea of the ownership of children by men, the raising of children in family instead of communal units, the origin of private property, the passing of private property down to children, the origin of marriage (which was really locking women up long enough to make sure who the father was) and in general the curtailment of women's freedom so that dynastic structures of various kinds could prevail—all these were results of a fundamental discovery.

So gradually, with our freedom restricted by systems of marriage and marked as physically, visibly different whether or not we had children, we became the first politically subjugated group—we were the means of production and our freedom had to be curtailed if male dynasties were to be secure. Gradually the pre-existing gynecocratic structures were replaced by a series of patriarchal ones. And as a subjugated second class group, we became also naturally the group that was given whatever work to do that was not rewarded by that society. We became a kind of cheap labor supply for whatever the tribe or the state may have demanded. We were given "feminine" or "women's" jobs, in other words, which can be defined as anything a man doesn't want to do—whether it's clerical work or ditch-digging just depends on the society.

When other groups that were marked by cultural or racial differences were captured and brought into these newly patriarchal structures, they, too, were given whatever repetitive or boring or difficult tasks that the ruling class did not wish to perform. Therefore, there always has been the closest kind of parallel between women in patriarchal societies and any other groups held to be biologically second class.

THE PARALLEL BETWEEN WOMEN AND BLACKS

According to Gunnar Myrdal, the deepest truth of American life is the parallel between women of all races and black men. Because we are the two largest second class groups. We are the inexpensive supply of labor on which the economic system depends.

Myrdal was not necessarily equating the suffering. Black women as well as black men may risk losing their lives, whereas white women more often lose their identities. But the mythology is the same. He pointed out some of the parallel myths: that women of all races and black men have been said to have smaller brains, passive natures, child-like natures; that we are thought to be incapable of governing ourselves. (Maybe we can be head of the secretarial pool. Maybe we can, if we're black reporters, report on the black community or maybe we can run advertising agencies that design products and ads especially for the black community. But the problem comes in when we have decision-making power over the lives of white men.)

There are many more parallel myths; that we're late all the time; we're irresponsible; we don't like to work for each other; and we don't get on well with each other. (Black people were supposed to not want to go to black professionals, for instance, and women, of course, were supposed to be so busy competing for the favors of the ruling class that we never can get together.) We're closer to the earth. We're more emotional. Our natures are more sexual. We have natural rhythm—with women it's lunar and with minority men it's musical.

Men have monthly cycles too, you know. In societies where people are less addicted than we are here to the myth of John Wayne and changeless masculinity, in Japan for instance, where they have an enormously high-speed and dangerous transportation system, they have required their male workers to figure out their monthly cycles and therefore to know on which days they are more accident prone. As a result, they've cut their accident rate in half.

The truth is that we're all on this earth, governed by the lunar cycle, whether we are males or females or potatoes or cats or whatever we are.

Let's see, what are the other myths? Well, according to television, there's even an idea that we have peculiar odors. And some of you have contributed to making us feel insecure about that fact, therefore building rather large and important manufacturing industries on that insecurity. I don't know how anybody who's ever passed a locker room can really believe that . . but . .

These are all parallel. Now that we have just barely begun to realize how very racist this society is, it's helpful to substitute the name of any group of men racially considered to be second class, and to see what it is that we are really saying when we make these generalized statements about women.

It's also important from an anthropological point of view to understand that these two kinds of caste systems have imitated each other, have developed together, and wherever one group is marked for discrimination, the other group is also being discriminated against. It doesn't matter whether it is Jews and women in Nazi Germany or women and blacks in South Africa or women and minority men in our own society. Wherever we find a great deal of racial discrimination, we will also find a great deal of discrimination against women. They are the most fundamental kinds of caste.

THE MYTH OF BIOLOGICAL INFERIORITY

Perhaps one of the deepest ways women of all races and black men are discriminated against is that our inferior positions are said to be somehow "natural." We are not doing well; therefore it must be somehow our fault. There are all those questions about where are all the great women painters, and chefs and so on. They all boil down to: If you're so smart, why aren't you rich? There's an assumption that the existing order is the natural one—and is justified by biology.

The World Health Organization did a study recently which was directed toward the discovery of sex-based differences in many different cultures. They could find no intellectual or emotional differences at all between males and females as groups. But what is even more surprising perhaps is that the difference in physical strength which we have grown culturally to feel is so great turned out to be "marginal" and "transitory." Transitory because it tends to exist only during the child-bearing years: that is, very old males and females and very young males and females have about the same degree of physical strength. And marginal because, even during the child-bearing years, the difference is not very great.

So we really have to question many of our assumptions about males and females as groups and to understand at last that, in fact, the generalized group differences between males and females—the differences of hormones and genitals—like the differences between two races of skin pigmentation, features and hair and so on, are operative for only very isolated functions: child-bearing on the one hand and resistance to certain diseases on the other.

But for the full range of human activities and functions, the individual differences are much, much greater than the group ones. In other words, the individual differences between any two women or two men in this room are likely to be greater for all functions other than childbirth than the generalized differences between males and females as groups.

It really only makes sense to base all of our job requirements and life expectations on the individual and never on the group. And that goes for all functions, including the raising of children.

RETURNING CHILDREN TO THEIR FATHERS

According to male logic, if a woman spends a year bearing and nurturing a child, then she must be more responsible than her husband for caring for that child until she or he gets to be self-sufficient. Well, women have made a very revolutionary discovery lately: a child has two parents.

So why isn't the man therefore responsible for spending that much more than half the time taking care of the child?

A great change that's happening is one that begins at the most basic level, one that is making alternatives in family structure, in life styles. One that is creating a new relationship between two adults who choose to have children and one that, far from depriving children of their mothers, is really concerned with returning children to their fathers; is really concerned with the fact that most American children suffer from much too much mother and too little father.

After all, in agricultural times, everybody worked together—aunts and uncles and cousins and grandmothers and children—near the house, and only industrialization really took the men away from the house for the first time—with suburbanization, very far away from the house—and ghettoized the wives and the children at home.

So we are beginning to search for a variety of alternatives, to create a system in which it is honorable to live alone, to live with a group, to live with another person, to have children or not to have children. We are beginning to lift up those crippling labels of "masculine" and "feminine" and to allow the individuality that is *human* to flower for the first time.

BLACK WOMEN ARE DOUBLY DISCRIMINATED AGAINST

There's another difference between women of all races and minority men in the ways that we are discriminated against. And that is that minority men are realistically perceived as powerless in this society, but women of all races are perceived as being already powerful. So we prolong the problem by the very neat device of pretending that no problem exists. We see black women, for instance, as matriarchs, but the truth is that a black woman with a B.A. degree who works full time makes less than a black man with an eighth grade education who works full time. She is suffering from the double discrimination of race and sex.

Black women are on the bottom of the economic ladder in terms of median income—with white women coming next, black men coming third, and white men on top.

As for white women, their myth of power is that they control the economy. And perhaps those of us here who sell to women as consumers may be even more subject to that myth because we are directed towards the one area in which women do have a statistical advantage, if one can call it an advantage: we do make most of the purchases at point of sale. That's true. But what kind of power is that?

It's comparable at best to the power we experience as voters. We can choose between Duz and Tide . . . between Humphrey and Nixon, but we very rarely have the power to determine among what objects or people the choice is made. Nor can we benefit either socially or economically from the choice once it is made.

WOMEN'S REAL ECONOMIC SITUATION

So we have to look at women's real economic situation. We're all full of ideas about rich widows traveling in Europe on their husband's insurance money and women living on alimony—but the constant attention to these statistical rarities is less proof of our great economic power than proof of the resentment of the little economic power that we actually do have.

It's interesting to look at the real statistics. Of all the women who get divorced in this country, fewer than 10% get any alimony at all. We see stories about enormous settlements, but the fact of the matter is that ten years after the divorce, 79% of the husbands are no longer making alimony payments—even to the less than 10% of ex-wives who were awarded it in the first place.

Then there's the question of child support. The average child support payment is less than half what is necessary to support a child. And that also diminishes in the same way so that even one year after a divorce, there are only about 38% of the fathers who are conforming. Women usually don't have the money or the resources to pursue their divorced husbands, especially if they've moved out of state, nor can they earn enough to support their kids. If she has children, even a woman with education and training may therefore end up on welfare.

Women live longer and therefore we're supposed to inherit all the wealth. Yes, we are two thirds of the beneficiaries for life insurance. But that does not address itself to how much the life insurance policy is, and whether it is designed to support children as well. Finally, it is rarely as much as a woman would have received had she been receiving even a minimal salary for the same number of years she's been working as a housewife and mother.

It's important to understand that work done in the home is real work. Men are always saying that the Movement is for women who work and by that they don't mean housewives. But housewives work harder than anybody. According to the Department of Labor, they work 99.6 hours a week and get no guaranteed pay for it. They also figured out that if a widower, for instance, has to pay for the services that the housewife performs, the average payment would be about $9,000 a year. Now how many housewives are receiving $9,000 a year for the services they are performing? The Department of Labor did not figure that out so that women would feel that they were performing important social functions. (Raising baby humans is an important social function, and somewhat more interesting than working in corporate structures perhaps.) They figured it out only so that the insurance companies would know how much to pay in damages to husbands whose wives had died.

Let's look at the stock market. Women are almost half of all the stockholders in the country, but in terms of the real dollar value of the stock that we own, it's about 38% and we, in fact, rarely control that stock. The New York Stock Exchange says that 75% of all the securities transactions are carried out by men. Women who own stock are far more likely to be sales people or clerical workers than men are, and to own only a few shares. Furthermore the stock in women's names is often used for the needs of the husband or children.

Then there's real estate. I guess we have to address that because we're supposed to inherit that too. Well, the IRS says that of all the people with $60,000 a year or more in total estate value, there are about two million men with $118 billion in real estate and one million women with about $69 billion in real estate. And again, most of it is in women's names, but not in women's control.

But maybe the best indicator is to say that among all the people in the country who earn or receive $10,000 a year or more in any form, less than 9% are women—and that includes all these famous rich widows. That's really where our economic power is at.

In terms of earned income it's even worse: of all the jobs that pay $15,000 a year or more, 94% are held by white males with 6%

left over for all women and minority men. Now, that's a statistic that I think really gives us some idea of what women's power is in this country.

And if you look at who is poor and who is not, you maybe get an even better idea. Because of course 85% of the people on welfare are women and dependent children. They're there because there's very little child care; alimony and support payments are poor as we've already seen; and women earn about 58% of what men do for fulltime work. I think it was best summed up by a woman I met who had been living in an upper middle class suburb, who had two years of college and three children and whose husband died. She had up to that time been very conservative politically and very anti welfare. But when her husband died and left her no money, she found that she could not get a job that would allow her even to pay enough to keep her children in child care centers. And so she ended up on welfare. And she said, "You know, the truth is that most women in the country are only *one man away from welfare.*"

Until we have a system in which every adult has the right to a decent wage, we are never going to solve the enormous problems of poverty.

WOMEN'S PLIGHT IS POLITICAL

It's difficult to get ourselves to look at the real situation instead of the mythological one. But once we do, once we understand finally what women's power really is and what our position really is, and once we see that this position is not natural, then we see that we can no longer quite ever feel the same about the world around us. We understand the nature of politics for the first time. It's not just something that goes on in the state capital or in Washington. It is any power relationship in our daily lives. Any time one group of people, or person, is habitually dominant over another group or person because of birth, because of caste or race or sex, not because of individual capability, that's politics.

That means that when we go into our offices now, and we see 70 of one kind of human typing and 12 of another in the boardroom, we understand that that's politics. When we pick up a telephone and we get a woman at the other end of the wire, and a disproportionate amount of the time it's a minority woman, and we know where they are in the structure of the telephone company, we see that's politics. When we look at advertising and we see that cleaning products and food are directed toward women, are shown only with women, we understand that that's politics. When we look at a marriage and see that both husband and wife are working outside the home, but the wife is still somehow more responsible for taking care of the children and getting dinner, that's a political, a power relationship. When we see a woman who has put her husband through graduate school and somehow the favor has never been returned, that's politics. Or a woman who is expected to move when her husband gets a better job offer, but his moving when she gets a better job offer is not even discussed, that's politics.

Then we look at the way we choose our business and political leadership. For the most part, we have eliminated women of every race . . . that's 53% right there . . . then minority men, then pretty much everybody who hasn't been able to buy a college education and everybody under thirty. When you're through with all that, you come out with 4½% of the country.

That's the enormous pool of talent from which we've been choosing our leadership. No wonder we're in such trouble.

WHAT THE CHANGES IN WOMEN'S STATUS WILL MEAN

We are just beginning to see the depth of change that we're really talking about . . . to see that it affects everything around us. It affects work patterns, because men will not have to work obsessively for forty years and end up with an engraved watch, or work eight hours a day and commute for another two hours, because there will be two sources of income in the home. Indeed, shared work may make the five-hour day or the three- or four-day week a very possible reality.

It means that the family structure will change, that buying patterns will change, that the way we sell our products will change, that architecture will change. There will be many fewer big settlements of ticky-tacky boxes very far away from the places of work, for instance, and more communal space—a whole different kind of urban organization and architecture. Forms of structure in the offices will change because hierarchical structure only imitates patriarchy anyway, which doesn't work at home or in the office.

The feminist revolution will change language—which is very patriarchal. It will change religion, which may be the champion myth-maker of all time. It will change politics because women do have a different voting pattern from men . . . not biologically different but culturally different. We identify with "out" groups whether or not it's done so consciously. It will change foreign policy which many political scientists are pointing out has been based on the masculine mystique, on machismo, on the need to win, or at the very least, never, never to admit failure. It will change everything that is around us and it is a change that is expected by many women. In the Harris poll of 1972, for the first time a plurality of American women expressed their support for the goals of the Women's Movement.

HOW WOMEN RESPOND TO ADVERTISING

Good Housekeeping conducted a survey of women's response to advertising, which I'm sure you know about. And 40% of the women they questioned said they found advertising directed at them "offensive." That's a lot. We knew that, perhaps, though we didn't know the full percentage. But what we did not know, and what we find at *Ms.*, is the amount of gratitude and loyalty and support that is offered to advertisers who do *not* suppose that women are restricted to supportive roles.

Who are we? Well, we're every woman who has ever stood by a kitchen sink with a B.A. degree or an M.A. degree wondering what the hell is going on . . . isn't there more to life than this? We are women on welfare who see the welfare system as a gigantic husband. We're every woman who has every been called upon to conceal her intelligence, who has ever been a victim of a double standard, sexual or economic, or who is a minority woman and therefore twice discriminated against.

We are literally all the individual women who have been struggling for so long to understand why we are in the positions we are in, who have been made to feel that it is our fault; that if we have 2.2 children and a very nice husband and we are not happy, there must be something wrong with us.

But there are men, too, who have realized their interest in these changes. Now, that's not to say that we really expect that men will give up their privileges voluntarily, as a group. I don't think that's happened so far in history. But we do understand that there are individual men who themselves see what's in it for them, who themselves see how much they have been restricted by the masculine role, by the whole idea that they have to earn a lot of money and be right all the time and not be with their children or not change their profession; who themselves understand that they're being dehumanized by those burdens.

There are those men who choose to fight this revolution along with women. And if it can be said that there is more virtue where there's more choice, then these men are more virtuous than women because they have a choice and choose to give up their masculine or their white skin privileges—to explore the whole range of human possibilities that should belong to them.

If you want to understand what women expect, the best advice that I can offer is this: consider what you would feel like if, with all the same hopes and dreams and ambitions that you have now as individual human beings, you had been born female. Then you will understand why we are angry and what we want individually and collectively and you'll also understand that this Movement is a very deep one, a very long term one and a very inevitable one. It doesn't matter whether there's a magazine or books or whether polls are taken or not: it is the most alive and far-reaching and forceful movement in the country. Nor is it confined to this country. It is part of a whole worldwide revolution against caste, against restriction by minor physical difference, whether it's race or sex.

Revolutionary feminism is the only path to humanism.

Thank you.

NATIONAL HEALTH INSURANCE—
OPPORTUNITY FOR ACTION NOW*

A Speech by
Leonard Woodcock†

As I look around this room I am again reminded of how wrong our society has been in setting an arbitrary age of 65 as a time for retirement. As millions of members who make up the National Council of Senior Citizens are demonstrating, the nation is the better for the dedicated responsibilities you are carrying out in public service not only in behalf of senior citizens but for all of us.

I am pleased to be here because I have known and admired your President, Nelson Cruikshank, for many years. He is an imaginative and able leader who changed his base of operations when he reached so-called retirement age but did not slow up the contributions he continues to make to progress in America.

I know I am talking to many of our own UAW members at this session. A majority of UAW retirees and their spouses are members of the 545 Retired Workers Chapters of our Union. These Chapters carry on varied, vigorous and often venturesome programs of which we are indeed proud. Some 14 years ago our retired workers recognized that large and influential as our program was becoming, it was not enough. Far greater strength could be gained through joining with others of similar interests in a national movement of senior citizens. We are therefore proud to acknowledge that we were one of the founding organizations in your National Council.

I want to talk with you today about health care but you would understand that it needs to be seen in the setting of our society and our approaches to dealing with the very severe problems we now face.

*Address to Legislative Conference of the National Council of Senior Citizens, Washington, D.C., June 9, 1975.

† Former president, International Union UAW; Chairman, Committee for National Health Insurance.

1. THE NEED FOR LEADERSHIP

President Harry S. Truman once said:

> In periods where there is no leadership, society stands still. Progress occurs when courageous, skillful leaders seize the opportunity to change things for the better.

I am deeply concerned that in the face of the most serious economic problems in three decades our executive branch is not showing the necessary leadership required to move this country. This may well be because of the philosophic commitment largely to leave the free forces of the marketplace to eventually work things out. The young people of our country are having a rebirth of nostalgia as they look back to the music and the customs of the 1950s. I sometimes wonder whether our national administration is not suffering similar nostalgia as they attempt to recapture the economic philosophy of the 1920s and 1930s.

I worry too about the Congress. The people elected a new, more forward looking Congress last fall. It consists of younger people, almost all of whom place a high premium on human values in contrast with the acquisition of material goods, and I am troubled that this new Congress has not yet found the means of developing the discipline and devising programs of leadership which are within their grasp, and which would deal with some of the pressing concerns our country now faces.

2. ECONOMIC ACTIONS

This country needs more stimulus to revive the economy and get us to a full employment situation. I think you will agree with me that we need to say as loudly and clearly as we can that a recovery which includes in its plans the continuing unemployment of more than eight million people by the end of 1976 is intolerable and unacceptable.

We need a large scale, imaginative program of public service employment for those who need work and cannot find it.

We need reform of the unemployment compensation system with the development of national standards, higher benefits, a longer period of eligibility for benefits, and uniform application of eligibility standards.

We require early adoption of a national energy program. That leadership I referred to earlier is required in bringing Congress and the Administration together in agreeing on a program rather than the wasting of energy in attempting to lay the blame on who is responsible for the absence of a program.

We do not face a crisis in our Social Security system. But we will have one in the next few years if we do not provide now for needed restructuring of its financing which is rapidly becoming outdated.

We need imaginative new programs to encourage public and private housing. We know that in each of the postwar recessions the recovery of the housing industry has helped lead this nation out of a recession.

3. NATIONAL ECONOMIC PLANNING

In citing but a few of the measures which need to be adopted to turn this country around, I have left to the end the long-range approach which would help us avoid in the future the type of instability and dislocations we are today experiencing. No reliable mechanism in the modern economy relates needs to available manpower, plant and materials. In consequence, we have shortages of housing, medical care, municipal services, transportation, energy and numerous other requirements of pressing importance. We have not made it our business to foresee these critical problems and take the steps to forestall them. But in a modern economy, planning is not a matter of preference or ideology. It is one of immediate need.

Senators Hubert Humphrey and Jacob Javitz have introduced in Congress a proposal developed by the Initiative Committee for National Economic Planning. It would create an Office of National Economic Planning which would be in a position to study our economic needs now and in the future. It would provide Congress and the executive branch with alternative plans for action—not only to predict hardship and disaster—but to guide the economy in a direction consistent with our national values and goals.

Almost every other industrialized and semi-industrialized nation has some sort of economic planning mechanism. The time is long past due for the United States to have this kind of mechanism which could read the signals and advise on the techniques for using our tremendous economic power to avoid recession after recession which so characterized post-World War II America.

4. THE HEALTH CARE SYSTEM

During the Depression of the 1930s we developed structures and mechanisms for the protection of families and workers which have kept things today from being a lot worse than they otherwise would have been. I am talking about programs such as Social Security and Unemployment Insurance, as well as job-creating programs which set the precedent for similar government action today.

Likewise, we should now seize the opportunity to develop new programs, not only to reduce the ill effects of future economic dislocations, but to improve the quality of life of all Americans here and now. One such urgently needed program is a system of national health insurance which guarantees to all Americans their right to a high quality of health care at a cost they can afford.

I know I do not need to tell a convention of senior citizens about the problems with our health care system. Eighty percent of you who are past the age of 65, and ninety percent of you who are over 70 experience some chronic medical condition. Forty-three percent of you, according to the government, have some limitation in activity. You see the doctor almost one-third more often than younger people. You are twice as likely to be hospitalized. And when you are in the hospital you remain some 50% longer than those in the general population.

Our goal as a society must not be simply to find more money for you to pay for longer and longer stays in hospitals and nursing homes. It must and can be to bring the achievements of modern medical science to bear on problems of the elderly to enable them to continue to function as contributing members of the society.

That's why we worked together to bring about the passage of Medicare ten years ago.

We knew the program was not perfect and expected that it

would be strengthened over time. But the river of history here runs backward. Medicare has been weakened and diluted, as you well can bear witness.

Today those over 65 are paying $179 *more* out of their own pockets for personal health care than they paid before they had the protection of Medicare. This is bitter prescription medicine for those on largely fixed incomes. Part B premiums have more than doubled, out of hospital prescription drugs are still not covered, physicians' fees have increased and participating physicians who accept assignment have dropped in six years from 60% to 50%.

You who fought for Medicare were asked to accept half a loaf. Through increased deductibles, co-payments and premiums, your half a loaf has had slice after slice taken out of it so that your share becomes less, and those who sell you services take more and more.

Many of those who oppose national health insurance are quick to point to the shortcomings of Medicare. In fact, Medicare is a much needed but inadequate form of national health insurance. It has enabled many without resources to get necessary care and it has kept others from being financially wiped out.

But it has done nothing to cure most of the basic ills of our health care system. This is because those who wrote it agreed to compromises which assured the doctors and the hospitals and those who stood to profit from Medicare that nothing in the legislation could be used to change the system of delivery of health care. But this is where the problem is. This is where we need to concentrate if we are to eliminate the shortcomings of Medicare and make access to decent health services a matter of right for each and every one of us in America.

It is not necessary for me to present you with a detailed cata-logue of the serious problems and weaknesses in our system of health care.

I have referred to the deficiencies in Medicare. You know all too painfully that the whole way in which we try to provide health in-surance is marked by gaps and overlaps, by fragmentation and con-fusion, and all too many Americans fall between the cracks. It is almost incomprehensible that after all these years, and in a year in which we spent $23 billion for private health insurance, 41 million Americans under the age of 65 have no private insurance coverage.

Heart-rending evidence of the ill effects of such fragmented coverage is shown in the case of the millions of laid-off American workers who not only face a loss of income but also a loss of health insurance coverage. When a worker is laid off he does not have to take his children out of public schools; and he does not lose his right to police and fire protection. Why must he and his family lose the equally basic right to coverage for the treatment of illness and injury? Thirty million Americans who are losing their work-related private health insurance coverage this year have a right to an answer to this question.

Another problem which is not new to any of us is the sky-rocketing inflation of the costs of health services. We spend twice as much per person as we did ten years ago, and health care prices are going up twice as fast as the Consumer Price Index.

Many are unable to gain access to the health care they need. Often this is because they are poor or don't have insurance. But all too often it is because there are not enough doctors where they live. And how many of you are sure you could get prompt and adequate medical care if you should need it at night or on a weekend?

And when we are able to get the health services we need, there is little way for us to know whether it meets the level of quality we have a right to expect. Even if the overall level of quality is good, the fact is that we hear of outrages almost every day which make us shudder. It is small wonder that we are facing a crisis in the area of medical malpractice insurance.

It was because of these familiar yet critical problems that we developed the proposal for National Health Security, which is sponsored by Senator Edward Kennedy and Congressman James Corman. It is designed to deal with these problems. That is why it enjoys the support of the National Council of Senior Citizens as well as the entire labor movement.

Of course many ask, why should we work for this Health Security program? Why don't we just expand and improve upon Medicare? Well the fact is that Medicare provides only insurance coverage, but does not deal with the problems of the health care delivery system. Medicare does not control costs; it does not improve quality; and it does not guarantee that the right kind of services will be available when needed.

Besides, we need a program which will guarantee the right to care for the whole population. Surely a sick five year old is just as entitled to receive care as a sick 70 year old. In addition, by including the whole population in a national health program, we follow the tested insurance principle once characterized by Winston Churchill as "The miracle of large numbers." The risk should be spread over the entire population, the young, the middle-aged and the elderly.

This is why the Health Security Program would cover the entire population. And Health Security would make coverage compulsory, like Social Security, so that those who have a lower risk will not opt out and leave the rest holding the high cost bag.

If we had such a universal program today we would not be faced with the grim specter of tens of millions losing their health coverage because the family breadwinner is out of work. Yet of the several national health insurance proposals now before Congress, only Health Security would prevent this dilemma. The others continue to rely upon employment-related coverage which has already proven to be disastrous.

Health Security also would make available fully paid benefits to cover the entire range of health services. No longer would senior citizens have to spend an average of $103 a year on necessary drugs. Regular physical exams would be covered. So would diagnostic services, as well as the treatment of illness in the appropriate setting. No more will you have to be put in the hospital unnecessarily because that was the only way the insurance would pay for it. And broad rehabilitation services would also be covered so that individuals could be restored to their maximum abilities. I stress this because the experts tell us large numbers of the elderly who are incapacitated need not be so, if timely rehabilitation services were available to them.

Under National Health Security there would be no more costly and unfair deductibles and co-payments. Right now those over 65 are paying over $400 a year out of their limited incomes for health care. It has been documented again and again that this deters many from seeking care they need. And how many here today have had to dig into your savings or go without other necessities so you could pay your medical bills? The Administration calls this "cost consciousness." I call it "regressive and discriminatory taxation." It constitutes lack of understanding or callous disregard of the real needs of old sick people.

Financing of coverage under Health Security would be simple and fair. It would use the tested and accepted mechanism of Social Security financing combined with federal general revenues. This is how the original designers of Social Security foresaw that national health insurance, as well as basic Social Security, would eventually be financed. Medicare taxes would be integrated with Health Security taxes. There would be no separate Medicare program because all Americans regardless of age would be covered by the much more comprehensive Health Security benefits.

Health Security would use the leverage of funds to deal with the disorganization and dislocations of the health services system. Through control of the budget, over a period of time enough doctors and the right kind of services would be available in every community, including inner-city neighborhoods and rural areas where so many of our elderly and our poor people live.

Special funds would be earmarked to increase resources for personal health services and to stimulate the development of new types of programs of service. For example, an area crying out for such special efforts is the outrageous situation which exists in our nursing homes.

Hundreds of thousands of chronically ill, most of them elderly, without access to decent extended health care or home health services, end up in the 22,000 nursing homes in our country. Ninety percent of the beds are operated first for profit, then for patients. Two Congressional investigations and any number of state probes have revealed the shame of nursing home operators who frequently neglect and often mistreat patients.

The New York State Health Department reported this past February there were "serious operating deficiencies in two-thirds of the nursing homes in New York City." In Connecticut last year almost half the proprietary nursing homes made profits of 50% or more for the year with some homes having profits as high as 286%. A spokesman for the Iowa Department of Health in describing conditions in nursing homes in his State, told the New York Times, "They're not saving lives. Most of their patients are dying. . . ."

How long must we continue to tolerate this terrible situation?

The facts have been known for at least a decade, and very, very little has been done to change the situation. It cries for immediate action which would include:

1. Tough uniform national quality standards under Medicare and Medicaid with ample enforcement funds.

2. A top level national consumer review group operating at the level of the Secretary of Health, Education and Welfare.

3. A mandated ombudsman mechanism in every major city.

4. Legislated requirements that in every nursing home with patients paid for with government funds, the patient or his next of kin have the right to see the medical record and to know the names and qualifications of persons giving care.

5. Statutory limitations on profits permissable for private nursing homes.

6. Subsidies to encourage the development of non-profit extended care facilities. A gradual phasing out of placement of government subsidized patients in "for profit" facilities.

This kind of program is one close to your hearts and interests. I hope you will press for its adoption now. At the same time you should know it would be far easier to achieve under the National Health Security Program your organization and I are advocating.

Taking a longer range view, we must begin to develop viable alternatives to long-term institutionalization. Hundreds of thousands of persons are in nursing homes today because more appropriate health care and supportive services are not available. The Kennedy-Corman Health Security Program is the only proposal for national health insurance which addresses this problem.

Under Health Security, grants would be made available to assist the development of community programs of comprehensive health and personal services designed to the maximum extent possible to keep elderly and infirm persons in their homes and with their families. These would include home maintenance services, laundry services, nutritional services such as meals on wheels, physical and occupational therapy, and assistance with transportation and shopping. In addition, measures are included to ensure the long range financing of those programs which are shown to be successful.

This is just another of many examples in which Health Security attempts to meet the needs of people, rather than forcing the people into patterns of care more convenient and profitable for providers of services and insurance companies.

Health Security would also take strong measures to attack the problem of substandard quality of care which is right now causing unnecessary hospitalizations, twice as much surgery as is needed, and countless adverse reactions to drugs which are administered inappropriately or without need. National standards for providers would be developed and implemented. And doctors and other professionals would have to periodically bring their knowledge and skills up to date in order to continue to participate in the program.

Consumer involvement would be instituted at every level of administration of Health Security. Organizations like the Senior Citizens would be assured a meaningful voice, and encouraged to develop community health care programs. Health care is too important a matter to leave even to the most enlightened professionals, let alone the special interests.

Public accountability for the system would be guaranteed by public administration. This would follow the tested experience of almost every other industrialized nation, including Canada. It would also end the current chaos with 1800 private insurance companies selling different policies and using different procedures, and each trying to skim off the top for themselves as much as possible.

It is clear that the Health Security Program presents the only real solution to our health care crisis. However, we often hear the claim made that we cannot afford Health Security, that we who support it are looking for a pie-in-the-sky free lunch. For the most part, such misleading statements are made by those who are managing to profit from our present health care problems and who would prefer the status quo to social progress. They come from the same school as those who used to claim that Social Security was the opening wedge to Socialism.

The fact of the matter is that we cannot afford not to enact Health Security. Every medical economist knows that there would be very little difference in the total costs of the various national health insurance proposals in the short run. But over a longer period of time, only Health Security has the built-in administrative, budget and cost controls to put a lid on national health expenditures. For example, to reduce hospital waste, hospitals would be given budgets that they would have to live with, just like you and I. And doctors would for the first time be held accountable for their fees and fee increases.

Without such measures, cost increases will continue on the rampage. Every year that we delay the enactment of Health Security means more billions of dollars wasted.

The Health Security Bill has more Congressional sponsors, 118 in this Congress, than it had in any previous Congress. We have a national coalition of labor unions, and consumer organizations, civil rights, fraternal, religious and youth groups at work. Thirty-five state committees are helping.

You, however, represent the grass roots power of this country. I urge you to go back to your clubs and to other local groups and begin a new and vigorous campaign for Health Security. Go up to the Hill before you leave town and make known your views. Deluge your Congressmen with letters and petitions calling for action, not more study and analysis. Tell them the answers we need can be found in the Kennedy-Corman Bill for National Health Security.

When I go to some of our Retired Workers Chapters, I see many of our members wearing hats and buttons proclaiming "Senior Power." I believe in Senior Power. I believe that Senior Power can make Health Security a reality.

A RECAPITULATION OF COURSE OBJECTIVES

This book has sought to guide you—

1. to a thorough understanding and awareness of the process of speech communication;
2. in the preparation and presentation of messages for public and private rhetorical situations;
3. in the development of increased critical thinking and listening skills;
4. to understand "dialogical communication" as an ideal orientation for meaningful speech communication;
5. to an awareness of the importance and usefulness of sound education in speech communication in the programs of higher education.

Suggested Speech Communication—Messages

1. *Personal Interest Message.* You select as a topic a major extracurricular interest or hobby; a labor of love that is especially meaningful and pleasurable in your life. You then prepare a message and select material to develop each line of thought for maximum impact on the others in class. The audience is to be recognized as being capable of listening with empathy, so that students can explore ideas and feelings with involvement and important ideas and attitudes in a credible and meaningful way.

2. *Issue Message.* This message brings into focus a public issue you believe should be of genuine concern to everyone in the class. You may wish to inform listeners about the existence of an issue they are apparently unaware of; you may wish to persuade them to view an issue in a certain way, or present ways to resolve it; or you may wish to get listeners to act in a certain way about an issue facing them. The source determines the goal and the specific purpose, and the issue is the central feature of the message. A full-content outline is required.

3. *Value Message.* Here you answer the question: If you had one speech to give, and five minutes to speak, what value would you talk about? The assignment is to be a very serious one. Why you have one speech to deliver is unimportant; what you choose to say is the only thing that really matters. You will have to search within yourself, your place in the world, and select something of value to answer the question for the assignment. This assignment can be among the most meaningful for both student and teacher in every instance. A full-content outline is required.

OBJECTIVES SHEET*
PERSONAL INTEREST MESSAGE

You engage in a dialogue of seven minutes in length. The first four to five minutes consists of a "Personal Interest" speech, and the remaining time is spent in a dialogue resulting from the speech.

The speech should focus on an interest or experience you have had, which you think would be of interest to the audience. An interest or experience can be further defined as a "hobby, . . . a labor of love, that is especially meaningful and pleasurable in your life."

The instructor usually expects each speaker to demonstrate competencies in the following areas:

1. Fulfilling the role of spokesperson in terms of coping with performance anxiety, effective delivery and having a clear purpose.
2. Strong identification with the topic of the message.
3. Obvious sensitivity or awareness of the audience and appropriate audience adaptation.

The audience is to be recognized as being capable of listening with empathy so that the students can explore ideas and feelings with involvement and honesty. This message encourages the student to project, via ego-involvement, important ideas and attitudes in a credible and meaningful way.

In addition, the following features of message preparation and presentation must be evident:

A. An introduction:
      which gains attention
      relates the subject to the specific audience
      states the central thought
B. A development:
      which explains the central thought
      which is logically organized
C. A conclusion:
      which summarizes

*The following pages have been reprinted from John J. Makay, ed., *Introduction to Rhetorical Communication: A Basic Coursebook* (Columbus: Collegiate Publishing Co., 1976). Used with permission.

emphasizes the central thought
gives the speech closure.

The instructor will also expect the student to demonstrate a proficiency in these areas of delivery:

A. Observation for feedback
B. Extemporaneous presentation
C. Appropriate body movement
D. Appropriate vocal variety
    1. volume
    2. rate
    3. pitch
    4. pauses
    5. pronunciation

This first speech communication assignment can be fulfilled most effectively by using an outline as a guide for speaking. Study the material below and use the information in your preparation of the Personal Interest Message.

What Should An Outline Look Like?

I. Introduction
    A. Gain attention
    B. Establish relationship
II. Main idea (core statement)
    A. Personal identification with the main idea
    B. Reason for presenting the idea
    C. Initial summary of subpoints
III. Body
    A. Subpoint
       (development)
    B. Subpoint
       (development)
    C. Subpoint
       (development)
IV. Conclusion
    A. Final summary
    B. Appropriate closure

In addition to this information, study the material on the use of visual aids.

VALUE MESSAGE

This is a five-minute presentation followed by a question-answer and critique period. This message will require you to turn in a full content outline on the day on which you are scheduled to speak. Values are psychologically based constructs which stem from primary beliefs you hold, and they serve unconsciously and/or consciously as standards for the guidance of approach-avoidance behavior. A value forms the basis for judgment and allows you to determine the importance of things and how you really feel. You may choose to present your personal value in one of a number of ways, depending upon your goal and specific purpose as a spokesperson, and depending upon how you view your audience. Again you will be required to serve effectively as a spokesperson, to be sensitive to your audience, to deliver your ideas with skill.

Remember: Guidelines for competencies can be drawn from the text, lecture notes, and the responses you gain from your classmates and instructor. Do yourself and your audience a favor— prepare yourself fully for handling this assignment.

Keep in mind that your message must be well organized, fully supported, and effectively delivered. Check yourself out on the items listed below:

1. Rhetorical goal?
2. Specific purpose?
3. Core statement?
4. Lines of reason?
5. Support?
6. Language?   In terms of meeting
7. Bodily movement?   the rhetorical
8. Gestural behavior?   situation
9. Vocal usage?
10. Timing?

In addition, the following features of message preparation and presentation must be evident:

A. An introduction:
    which gains attention
    relates the subject to the specific audience
    states the central thought

B. A development:
   which explains the central thought
   which is logically organized
C. A conclusion:
   which summarizes
   emphasizes the central thought
   gives the speech closure.

The instructor will also expect you to *demonstrate a proficiency* in these areas of delivery:

A. Observation for feedback
B. Extemporaneous presentation
C. Appropriate body movement
D. Appropriate vocal variety
   1. volume
   2. rate
   3. pitch
   4. pauses
   5. pronunciation

ISSUE MESSAGE

You prepare and deliver a five-minute message which deals with an *issue* of vital importance to you and your audience. Your preparation and presentation should clearly demonstrate your proficiency in speech communication as described and indicated in our texts, lectures, and section instruction at this point in the course. A question-answer period and oral criticism usually takes place following your presentation. *An issue is an important question centered in a problem which you and your audience need to face.* You may choose to deal solely with the question itself or you may choose to develop the question and present a solution to the issue as well. The issue may deal with a fact, value, or policy, but the *central concern* for you and your audience is facing the issue! You will be required to serve as an effective spokesperson, to reveal audience analysis and adaptation; to use effective delivery; and to present meaningful and sound organization, support, reasoning, and language.

In addition, the following features of message preparation and presentation must be evident:

1. An introduction:
   which gains attention
   relates the subject to the specific audience
   states the central thought
2. Development:
   which explains the central thought
   which is logically organized, carefully reasoned, supported,
   and organized
3. A conclusion:
   which summarizes
   emphasizes the central thought
   gives the speech closure.

ASSIGNMENT_____

NAME_____

TOPIC_____

105 CRITIQUE

		NOT APPARENT	POOR	AVERAGE	ABOVE AVERAGE	EXCELLENT	INSTRUCTOR COMMENTS
I. **Content**	I.						
A. Was the speaker a strong spokesperson?	A.						
B. Organization, Support, Reasoning	B.						
1. Introduction	1.						
a. Gained attention	a.						
b. Adapted subject to specific audience	b.						
c. Stated the central thought	c.						
2. Body	2.						
a. Explained the central thought	a.						
b. Logically organized	b.						
1. Development of major points	1.						
2. Transitions	2.						
3. Support	3.						
3. Conclusion	3.						
a. Summarized speech	a.						
b. Emphasized central thought	b.						
c. Gave speech closure	c.						
C. Was the specific purpose (response) achieved?	C.						
D. Was the language meaningful and appropriate?	D.						
E. Was a dialogic atmosphere developed?	E.						
F. Did the topic meet the assignment?	F.						
II. **Delivery**	II.						
A. Observation for feedback	A.						
B. Extemporaneous presentation	B.						
C. Appropriate bodily movement	C.						
D. Appropriate vocal variety	D.						
1. Volume	1.						
2. Rate	2.						
3. Pitch	3.						
4. Pronunciation	4.						

PUBLIC SPEECH COMMUNICATION CRITIQUE

GOAL: Continuance, Discontinuance, Deterrence, or Adoption

Speaker's Name_____ Title_____

Date_____ Evaluator's Name_____

C H A R T

TOPICS	WEAK	FAIR	GOOD	EXCELLENT
A. Quality of Ideas				
B. Definition of Purpose				
C. Analysis of Subject				
D. Adaptation to Audience				
E. Language Style				
F. Posture and Physical Action				
G. Voice				
H. Visual Directness				
I. Self-Management				
J. Communication				

COMMENTS: Grade_____

PUBLIC SPEECH COMMUNICATION CRITIQUE

GOAL: Expository or Pleasure

Speaker's Name_____   Title_____

Date_____   Evaluator's Name_____

C H A R T

TOPICS	WEAK	FAIR	GOOD	EXCELLENT
A. Quality of Ideas				
B. Definition of Purpose				
C. Analysis of Subject				
D. Adaptation to Audience				
E. Language Style				
F. Posture and Physical Action				
G. Voice				
H. Visual Directness				
I. Self-Management				
J. Communication				

COMMENTS: Grade_____

Selected Books for Additional Reading

1. Applbaum, Ronald L. and Karl W. E. Anatol, *Strategies for Persuasive Communication*. Columbus: Charles E. Merrill Publishing Company, 1974. This is a basic, sound, and highly readable introduction to persuasion which focuses on attitudes, persuasion as a process, and strategies for persuasion.

2. Barnhart, Sara A. *Introduction to Interpersonal Communication*. New York: Thomas Y. Crowell Co., 1976. An excellent companion to our book. Instead of a concern for speaking with an audience, it focuses on one-to-another transactions and treats channels of communication, perception, language, nonverbal communication, self-concept, and patterns of communication.

3. Bettinghaus, Erwin P. *Persuasive Communication*, 2nd ed. New York: Holt, Rinehart, and Winston, Inc. 1973. A good basic text in theories of persuasion; and it is somewhat more comprehensive than the first book listed.

4. Crable, Richard E. *Argumentation as Communication: Reasoning With Receivers*. Columbus: Charles E. Merrill Publishing Company, 1976. A fresh approach to the study and practice of argument with useful case studies for purposes of application. The Toulmin approach is treated in detail and with clarity.

5. DeVito, Joseph A. *Communication: Concepts and Processes* (revised and enlarged). Englewood Cliffs, New Jersey: Prentice-Hall, Inc., 1976. A collection of materials about human communication. You can find twenty-

eight selections which provide comprehensive study and a lively variety of points of view.

6. Holland, DeWitte, ed. *America in Controversy: History of American Public Address*. Dubuque: Wm. C. Brown Company Publishers, 1973. This book consists of twenty-four original essays about public speaking in America from the Colonial Period through the 1960's Peace Movement and Vietnam War. One way to learn about speaking with an audience is to study the role of rhetorical communication in the growth of our society. This is a good book.

7. King, Robert G. *Forms of Public Address*. Indianapolis: The Bobbs-Merrill Company, Inc., 1969. For a brief introduction to public speaking in terms of deliberative, ceremonial, and entertaining speeches, this small paperback is good. It is very basic and practical for the development of speaking skill.

8. Linkugel, Wil A., R. R. Allen, and Richard L. Johannesen, *Contemporary American Speeches*. Belmont, California: Wadsworth Publishing Company, Inc. This small paperback offers a study of public speaking through the use of selected speeches under the categories of informative discourse, persuasive discourse, and ceremonial discourse. All of the speeches in this collection were aimed at one or more of the general objectives developed in our text. The analysis of the speeches and the speeches themselves provide excellent reading.

9. Johannesen, Richard L. *Ethics in Human Communication*. Columbus: Charles E. Merrill Publishing Company, 1975. There are only a few books in the field of Communication which deal sharply with ethical perspectives. This paperback is one of them. It speaks of public confidence, ethical responsibility, and other important topics for the communicator, and it offers issues and examples for analysis and discussion.

10. Makay, John J. and William R. Brown, *The Rhetorical Dialogue: Contemporary Concepts & Cases*. Dubuque: Wm. C. Brown Company Publishers, 1972. A unique book which provides an equal balance between concepts in rhetorical communication and examples by a variety of public communicators, most of them familiar to us all. The need for dialogue, the rhetorical purposes, audience images, self-projection, support, reasoning, and organization, and language are treated with care, and each chapter provides several complete texts of speeches for student application.

11. Makay, John J. *Exploration in Speech Communication*. Columbus: Charles E. Merrill Publishing Co., 1973. A collection of 21 essays ranging from an introduction to speech communication to intrapersonal and interpersonal communication to public speech communication. For a good survey of literature from a variety of writers, this text is valuable.

12. ———. *Introduction to Rhetorical Communication: A Basic Coursebook*. Columbus: Collegiate Publishing Co., 1976. Another collection of

materials for speaking with an audience. There are 16 selections from the writing of a variety of scholars; there are speech activities used with success; and there are discussion/critique forms for the evaluation of speaker performance. The book contains good supplementary materials for an introductory course.

13. ————., and Beverly A. Gaw. *Personal and Interpersonal Communication: Dialogue with the Self and with Others.* Columbus: Charles E. Merrill Publishing Co., 1976. This book is quite different from the text. For the person who wants to explore theory and cases in intrapersonal and interpersonal communication, and compare and contrast this information with material about public speaking, this is an excellent introduction.

14. Mudd, Charles S., and Malcolm O. Sillars. *Speech: Content and Communication.* 3rd ed. New York: Thomas Y. Crowell Co., 1975. An extremely comprehensive paperback heavily oriented to traditional public speaking, but which includes good information on interpersonal interaction and small group communication. Our text has drawn several pieces of information from this book.

15. Oliver, Robert T. *History of Public Speaking in America.* Boston: Allyn & Bacon, 1965. A second excellent book on public speaking in America, it is different from Holland's book in that it is a single-author text and it concludes with events in the early part of this century.

16. Thompson, Wayne N. *Quantitative Research in Public Address and Communication.* New York: Random House, 1967. A reasonably comprehensive review of the findings of experimental research up through the mid-1960s. For those interested in looking at theory from a quantitative perspective and considering these findings with those in historical-critical research, this is a valuable book. A student new to the study and practice of public speaking may need some assistance in handling the language and procedures of social science.

INDEX

Attitudes, 63–64
Audience adaptation, 54–58, 162
Audience analysis, 71–76
Audience psychology, 62
Audience types, 77–80
Beliefs, 64–67
Causes of speech tension, 25–28
Communication models, 5–11
Conclusions in speaking, 143
Control of speech tension, 28–29

Core idea, 86
Course objectives, 4, 201
Delivery, 35–43
Distractions, 37
Dialogue, 45–46
Entitlement in language, 168
Ethics, 45–48
Ethos, 43–45
Evaluation forms, 210
Goals in communication, 11
Information processing, 59–62

Informative speaking, 12
Introductions in speaking, 142
Language, 156, 164–165
Language use suggestions, 170–172
Library use, 105–120
Meaning, 8
Monologue, 45–46
Nonverbal communication, 31–34
Note taking, 120
Organization of ideas, 139–140
Organizational models, 144–147
Outlining, 148–152
Perception, 6–7

Persuasive discourse, 12
Propositions, 86–89
Reasoning defined, 130
Research, 105
Rhetoric, 10–11
Self-confidence, 9
Self-image and language, 161
Speech assignments, 176, 201–206
Speech tension, 22–29
Supporting material, 89–98
Symbol referent thought, 157–158
Toulmin approach, 130–138
Values, 67–70
Visual support, 99–104
Voice, 38–43
Word choice, 167–168

77 78 79 80 81 7 6 5 4 3 2